CAREERS FOR

PATRIOTIC TYPES

& Others Who Want to Serve Their Country

Careers for You Series

CAREERS FOR PATRIOTIC TYPES

& Others Who Want to Serve Their Country

JAN GOLDBERG

SECOND EDITION

McGraw-Hill

New York Chicago San Francisco Lisbon London Madrid Mexico City Milan New Delhi San Juan Seoul Singapore Sydney Toronto

The McGraw-Hill Companies

Library of Congress Cataloging-in-Publication Data

Goldberg, Jan.
Careers for patriotic types & others who want to serve their country / by Jan Goldberg — 2nd ed.
p. cm. — (McGraw-Hill careers for you series)
ISBN 0-07-144862-4 (alk. paper)
1. Vocational guidance—United States. I. Title: Careers for patriotic types and others who want to serve their country. II. Title. III. Series.

HF5382.5.U5G646 2006
331.702—dc22 2005002528

1 2 3 4 5 6 7 8 9 0 DOC/DOC 0 9 8 7 6 5

ISBN 0-07-144862-4

This book is printed on acid-free paper.

This book is dedicated to the memory of my beloved parents, Sam and Sylvia Lefkovitz, and the memory of a dear uncle, Bernard Lefko.

Contents

	Acknowledgments	ix
CHAPTER ONE	**Is the Patriotic Path Right for You?**	1
CHAPTER TWO	**Careers in Law Enforcement**	5
CHAPTER THREE	**Careers in Firefighting and Emergency Medical Services**	41
CHAPTER FOUR	**Careers in the Military**	59
CHAPTER FIVE	**Careers in Politics and Government**	87
CHAPTER SIX	**Careers on Foreign Soil**	117
CHAPTER SEVEN	**Careers in Space**	143

Acknowledgments

The author gratefully acknowledges the numerous professionals who graciously agreed to be profiled in this book and the following:

- My dear husband, Larry, for his inspiration and vision
- My children—Sherri, Deborah, and Bruce—for their encouragement and love
- Family and close friends—Adrienne, Marty, Mindi, Cary, Michele, Paul, Michele, Alison, Steve, Marci, Steve, Brian, Steven, Jesse, Bertha, and Aunt Helen—for their faith and support
- Diana Catlin, for her insights and input

The editors would like to thank Josephine Scanlon for revising this second edition.

Acknowledgments

CHAPTER ONE

Is the Patriotic Path Right for You?

Ask not what your country can do for you;
ask what you can do for your country.
—John F. Kennedy

Does the John F. Kennedy quote above call out to you? This is one of the sayings for which the late President Kennedy is most famous, perhaps because so many have recognized its relevance in their own lives.

For many, the feelings expressed above strike a chord. The patriotic spirit is very strong in these individuals, and many feel that the best way to carry out this sentiment is through career choice. And that's where this book comes in. It describes a wide range of occupations that allow you to express the patriotic spirit in your heart.

Is the patriotic path right for you? Take the following test and you'll find out!

The Patriotic Quiz

1. Do you have an especially strong feeling of allegiance to your country?
2. Would you be willing to relocate to another part of the country or even the world?

3. Could you adjust to unconventional work schedules?
4. Are you confident in your abilities?
5. Do you have a willingness to serve others and your country?
6. Do you enjoy meeting and dealing with many kinds of people?
7. Are you flexible about living conditions—possibly difficult ones?
8. Are you comfortable with an element of danger in your work?
9. Are you willing to make great sacrifices for your country and your fellow men and women?
10. Are you willing to risk your own well-being for the well-being of others?

A Tradition of Patriotism

In a large number of cases, patriotism seems to run in families. Did you know about these presidents' children who also served in the government?

- John Quincy Adams—son of John Adams: minister to the Netherlands from 1794 to 1796, minister to Germany from 1796 to 1801, senator for Massachusetts from 1803 to 1808, minister to St. Petersburg from 1809 to 1811, negotiator of the Treaty of Ghent in 1814, minister to Great Britain from 1815 to 1817, secretary of state from 1817 to 1825, president from 1825 to 1829, representative for Massachusetts from 1831 to 1848
- Charles Francis Adams—son of John Quincy Adams: representative from Massachusetts from 1859 to 1861, minister to Great Britain from 1861 to 1868
- John Scott Harrison—son of William Henry Harrison: representative from Virginia from 1893 to 1897

- Robert Todd Lincoln—son of Abraham Lincoln: secretary of war from 1881 to 1885, minister to Great Britain from 1889 to 1893
- James Rudolph Garfield—son of James Garfield: secretary of the interior from 1907 to 1909
- Theodore Roosevelt Jr.—son of Theodore Roosevelt: assistant secretary of the navy from 1921 to 1924, governor of Puerto Rico from 1929 to 1932, governor general of the Philippines from 1932 to 1933
- Robert Alphonso Taft—son of William Howard Taft: senator from Ohio from 1939 to 1953
- Charles Phelps Taft—son of William Howard Taft: mayor of Cincinnati from 1955 to 1957
- Herbert Hoover Jr.—son of Herbert Hoover: undersecretary of state for Middle Eastern affairs from 1954 to 1957
- Franklin Delano Roosevelt Jr.—son of F.D.R.: congressman from New York from 1949 through 1955, undersecretary of commerce from 1963 to 1965, chairman of the Equal Employment Opportunity Commission from 1965 to 1966
- James Roosevelt—son of F.D.R.: representative from California from 1955 to 1965
- Elliott Roosevelt—son of F.D.R.: mayor of Miami Beach from 1965 to 1967
- George W. Bush—son of George H. W. Bush: governor of Texas from 1995 to 2000, president from 2001 to 2004, reelected to serve until 2008
- John Ellis (Jeb) Bush—son of George H. W. Bush: governor of Florida from 1999 to 2002, reelected in 2002, to serve until 2007

Fathers and Daughters

Several women also followed their fathers in serving the nation as senators and representatives.

- Ruth Hanna McCormick—daughter of Senator Mark Hanna: representative from Illinois from 1929 to 1931
- Ruth Bryan Owen—daughter of William Jennings Bryan: representative from Florida from 1929 to 1933
- Clare Boothe Luce—stepdaughter of Representative Albert E. Austin: representative from Connecticut from 1943 to 1947
- Louise Goff Reece—daughter of Senator Guy Despard Goff: representative from Tennessee from 1961 to 1963
- Lucille Roybal-Allard—daughter of Representative Edward Roybal: representative from California since 1993
- Susan Molinari—daughter of Representative Guy Molinari: representative from New York from 1990 to 1997

Perhaps you will be the one in your family to initiate this patriotic trend. Or you may follow in the footsteps of other family members who have already entered one of the patriotic fields—law enforcement, firefighting, the Peace Corps, the military, politics, or government. All of these areas are open to patriotic souls.

The Patriotic Essence

The essence of patriotism was clearly expressed by President Dwight D. Eisenhower in words attributed as his last: "I've always loved my wife. I've always loved my children. I've always loved my grandchildren. And I have always loved my country."

CHAPTER TWO

Careers in Law Enforcement

The execution of the laws is more important than the making of them.
—Thomas Jefferson

In light of world events, Americans are more concerned than ever before with the need to reduce serious crime through law enforcement. In response to this concern, law enforcement officers are more visible and involved in communities, whether high-crime urban neighborhoods or quiet suburbs. This increased presence serves to increase public confidence in the police and mobilizes the public to help police fight crime. The national focus on reducing crime and increasing public safety also means that the jobs of correctional officers, who maintain order within jails and prisons, are more important than ever.

Law Enforcers

People depend on police officers and detectives to protect their lives and property. Law enforcement officers, some of whom are state or federal special agents or inspectors, perform these duties in a variety of ways, depending on the size and type of their organizations. In most jurisdictions, they are expected to exercise authority when necessary, whether on or off duty.

Police Officers

Uniformed police officers who work in municipal police departments, small communities, and rural areas have general law enforcement duties including maintaining regular patrols and responding to calls for service. They may direct traffic at the scene of a fire, investigate a burglary, or give first aid to an accident victim. In large police departments, officers usually are assigned to a specific type of duty. Many urban police agencies are becoming more involved in community policing, a practice in which an officer builds relationships with the citizens of local neighborhoods and mobilizes the public to help fight crime.

Police agencies are usually organized into geographic districts, with uniformed officers assigned to patrol a specific area, such as part of the business district or an outlying residential neighborhood. Officers may work alone, but in large agencies they often patrol with a partner. While on patrol, officers attempt to become thoroughly familiar with their patrol areas and remain alert for anything unusual. Suspicious circumstances and hazards to public safety are investigated or noted, and officers are dispatched to individual calls for assistance within their districts. During their shifts, they may identify, pursue, and arrest suspected criminals; resolve problems within the community; and enforce traffic laws.

Public college and university police forces, public school district police, and agencies serving transportation systems and facilities are examples of special police agencies. These agencies have specific geographic jurisdictions or enforcement responsibilities in the United States. Most sworn personnel in special agencies are uniformed officers; a smaller number are investigators.

Some police officers specialize in such diverse fields as chemical and microscopic analysis, training and firearms instruction, or handwriting and fingerprint identification. Others work with special units such as horseback, bicycle, motorcycle, or harbor patrol; canine corps; or special weapons and tactics (SWAT) or emergency response teams. A few local and special law enforcement officers primarily perform jail-related duties or work in courts. Regardless of job duties or location, police officers and detectives at all levels must write reports and maintain meticulous records that will be needed if they testify in court.

Sheriffs and Deputy Sheriffs

Sheriffs and deputy sheriffs enforce the law on the county level, working in rural communities and areas that do not have their own police departments. Sheriffs are usually elected to their posts and perform duties similar to those of a local or county police chief.

Sheriff's departments are generally relatively small, most having fewer than twenty-five sworn officers. A deputy sheriff in a large agency has law enforcement duties similar to those of officers in an urban police department. Police and sheriff's deputies who provide security in city and county courts are sometimes called bailiffs.

State Police Officers

State police officers (sometimes called state troopers or highway patrol officers) arrest criminals statewide and patrol highways to enforce motor vehicle laws and regulations. Uniformed officers are probably best known for issuing traffic citations to drivers who violate the law. At the scene of an accident, they may direct traffic, give first aid, and call for emergency equipment. Troopers also write reports used to determine the cause of an accident. State police officers are frequently called upon to render assistance to other law enforcement agencies, especially those in rural areas or small towns.

State law enforcement agencies operate in every state except Hawaii. Most full-time sworn personnel are uniformed officers who regularly patrol and respond to calls for service. Others are investigators, perform court-related duties, or work in administrative or other assignments.

Detectives

Detectives are plainclothes investigators who gather facts and collect evidence for criminal cases. Some are assigned to interagency task forces to combat specific types of crime. They conduct interviews, examine records, observe the activities of suspects, and participate in raids or arrests.

Detectives and state and federal agents and inspectors usually specialize in one of a wide variety of violations, such as homicide or fraud. They are assigned cases on a rotating basis and work on them until an arrest and conviction occurs or the case is dropped.

Federal Agents

The federal government maintains a high profile in many areas of law enforcement. Following are descriptions of the major federal agencies.

Federal Bureau of Investigation (FBI). FBI agents are the government's principal investigators, responsible for investigating violations of more than 260 statutes and conducting sensitive national security investigations. Agents may conduct surveillance, monitor court-authorized wiretaps, examine business records, investigate white-collar crime, track the interstate movement of stolen property, collect evidence of espionage activities, or participate in sensitive undercover assignments. The FBI investigates organized crime, public corruption, financial crime, fraud against the government, bribery, copyright infringement, civil rights violations, bank robbery, extortion, kidnapping, air piracy, terrorism, espionage, interstate criminal activity, drug trafficking, and other violations of federal statutes.

U.S. Drug Enforcement Administration (DEA). DEA agents enforce laws and regulations relating to illegal drugs. Not only is the DEA the lead agency for domestic enforcement of federal drug laws, it also has sole responsibility for coordinating and pursuing

U.S. drug investigations abroad. Agents may conduct complex criminal investigations, carry out surveillance of criminals, and infiltrate illicit drug organizations using undercover techniques.

U.S. Marshals and Deputy Marshals. These law enforcement officers protect the federal courts and ensure the effective operation of the judicial system. They provide protection for the federal judiciary, transport federal prisoners, protect federal witnesses, and manage assets seized from criminal enterprises. They have the widest jurisdiction of any federal law enforcement agency and are involved to some degree in nearly all federal law enforcement efforts. In addition, U.S. marshals pursue and arrest federal fugitives.

U.S. Immigration and Naturalization Service (INS). INS agents and inspectors facilitate the entry of legal visitors and immigrants to the United States and detain and deport those arriving illegally. The INS includes border-patrol agents, immigration inspectors, criminal investigators, immigration agents, and detention and deportation officers. U.S. Border Patrol agents protect more than eight thousand miles of international land and water boundaries. Their missions are to detect and prevent the smuggling and unlawful entry of undocumented foreign nationals into the United States, to apprehend those persons found in violation of the immigration laws, and to intercept contraband, such as narcotics. Immigration inspectors interview and examine people seeking entrance to the United States and its territories. They inspect passports to determine whether people are legally eligible to enter the United States. Immigration inspectors also prepare reports, maintain records, and process applications and petitions for immigration or temporary residence.

Customs and Border Protection. Customs agents investigate violations of narcotics smuggling, money laundering, child pornography, customs fraud, and enforcement of the Arms Export Control Act. Domestic and foreign investigations involve the development and use of informants, physical and electronic surveillance, and examination of records from importers and exporters, banks, couriers, and manufacturers. They conduct interviews, serve on joint task forces with other agencies, and obtain and execute search warrants.

To enforce laws governing imports and exports, customs inspectors inspect cargo, baggage, and articles worn or carried by people and carriers including vessels, vehicles, trains, and aircraft entering or leaving the United States. They seize prohibited or smuggled articles; intercept contraband; and apprehend, search, detain, and arrest violators of U.S. laws.

Bureau of Alcohol, Tobacco, Firearms, and Explosives (ATF). These agents regulate and investigate violations of federal firearms and explosives laws, as well as federal alcohol and tobacco tax regulations.

U.S. Secret Service. These special agents protect the president, vice president, and their immediate families; presidential candidates; former presidents; and foreign dignitaries visiting the United States. Secret Service agents also investigate counterfeiting, forgery of government checks or bonds, and fraudulent use of credit cards.

Bureau of Diplomatic Security. These special agents working for the U.S. Department of State are engaged in the battle against terrorism. Overseas, they advise ambassadors on all security matters and manage a complex range of security programs designed to protect personnel, facilities, and information. In the United States, they investigate passport and visa fraud, conduct personnel security investigations, issue security clearances, and protect the secretary of state and a number of foreign dignitaries. They also train foreign civilian police and administer a counterterrorism reward program.

Other Federal Agencies. Police and special agents with sworn arrest powers and the authority to carry firearms are also employed by other federal agencies. These agencies include the U.S. Postal Service, the Bureau of Indian Affairs Office of Law Enforcement, the U.S. Forest Service, the National Park Service, and the Federal Air Marshals.

Working Conditions

Police work can be very dangerous and stressful. In addition to the obvious dangers of confrontations with criminals, officers need to be constantly alert and ready to deal appropriately with a number of other threatening situations. Many law enforcement officers witness death and suffering resulting from accidents and criminal behavior. A career in law enforcement may take a toll on officers' private lives.

Uniformed officers, detectives, agents, and inspectors are usually scheduled to work forty-hour weeks, but paid overtime is common. Shift work is necessary because protection must be provided around the clock. Junior officers frequently work weekends, holidays, and nights. Police officers and detectives are required to work at any time their services are needed and may work long hours during investigations. In most jurisdictions, officers are expected to be armed and to exercise their arrest authority whenever necessary, even if off duty.

The jobs of some federal agents, such as U.S. Secret Service and DEA special agents, often require extensive travel on short notice. Agents may relocate a number of times over the course of their careers. Some special agents in agencies such as the U.S. Border Patrol work outdoors in rugged terrain for long periods and in all kinds of weather.

Qualifications and Training

Police Officers

Civil service regulations govern the appointment of police and detectives in practically all states, large municipalities, and special police agencies, as well as in many smaller ones. Candidates must be United States citizens, usually at least twenty years of age, and must meet rigorous physical and personal qualifications. In the federal government, candidates must be at least twenty-one years of age but less than thirty-seven years of age at the time of appointment. Physical examinations for entrance into law enforcement often include tests of vision, hearing, strength, and agility. Eligibility for appointment usually depends on previous education and experience as well as performance on competitive written examinations.

In larger departments, where the majority of law enforcement jobs are found, applicants usually must have at least a high school education. Federal and state agencies typically require a college degree. Candidates should enjoy working with people and meeting the public.

Law enforcement candidates are generally interviewed by senior officers to judge their honesty, sound judgment, integrity, and sense of responsibility. Candidates' character traits and backgrounds are investigated as well. In some agencies, candidates are interviewed by a psychiatrist or a psychologist or given a personality test. Most applicants are subjected to lie detector examinations or drug testing. Some agencies subject sworn personnel to random drug testing as a condition of continuing employment.

Before their first assignments, officers usually go through a period of training. In state and large local departments, recruits get training in their agency's police academy, often for twelve to fourteen weeks. In small agencies, recruits often attend a regional or state academy. Training includes classroom instruction in constitutional law and civil rights, state laws and local ordinances, and accident investigation. Recruits also receive training and supervised experience in patrol, traffic control, use of firearms, self-defense, first aid, and emergency response.

Police departments in some large cities hire high school graduates who are still in their teens as police cadets or trainees. They do clerical work and attend classes, usually for one to two years, at which point they reach the minimum age requirement and may be appointed to the regular force.

Police officers usually become eligible for promotion after a probationary period ranging from six months to three years. In a large department, promotion may enable an officer to become a detective or specialize in one type of police work, such as working with juveniles. Promotions to corporal, sergeant, lieutenant, and captain usually are made according to a candidate's position on a promotion list, as determined by scores on a written examination and on-the-job performance.

Federal Agents

Candidates for positions in all federal agencies must be U.S. citizens at least twenty-one years of age but less than thirty-seven when appointed.

To be considered for appointment as an FBI agent, an applicant must either be a graduate of an accredited law school or a college graduate with a major in accounting, fluency in a foreign language, or three years of related full-time work experience. All new agents undergo sixteen weeks of training at the FBI Academy on the U.S. Marine Corps base in Quantico, Virginia.

Applicants for special agent jobs with the U.S. Secret Service and the Bureau of Alcohol, Tobacco, Firearms, and Explosives must have a bachelor's degree or a minimum of three years of related work experience. Prospective special agents undergo ten weeks of initial criminal investigation training at the Federal Law Enforcement Training Center in Glynco, Georgia, and another seventeen weeks of specialized training with their particular agencies.

Candidates for special agent jobs with the U.S. Drug Enforcement Administration (DEA) must have a college degree and either one year of experience conducting criminal investigations, one year of graduate school, or have achieved at least a 2.95 grade point average while in college. DEA special agents undergo fourteen weeks of specialized training at the FBI Academy in Quantico, Virginia.

U.S. Border Patrol agents must be United States citizens, under thirty-seven years of age at the time of appointment, possess a valid driver's license, and pass a three-part examination on reasoning and language skills. A bachelor's degree or previous work experience that demonstrates the ability to handle stressful situations, make decisions, and take charge is required for a position as a border patrol agent. Applicants may qualify through a combination of education and work experience.

Training for All Candidates

Law enforcement agencies encourage applicants to take postsecondary school training in law enforcement–related subjects. Many entry-level applicants for police jobs have completed some formal postsecondary education and a significant number are college graduates. Many junior colleges, colleges, and universities offer programs in law enforcement or justice administration. Other valuable courses include accounting, finance, electrical engineering, computer science, and foreign languages. Physical education and sports are helpful in developing the competitiveness, stamina, and agility needed for many law enforcement positions. Knowledge of a foreign language is an asset in many federal agencies and urban departments.

Continuing training helps police officers, detectives, and special agents improve their job performance. Training is usually offered by police department academies, regional centers for public safety established by the states, and federal agency training centers. Instructors provide annual training in self-defense tactics, firearms, use-of-force policies, sensitivity and communications skills, crowd-control techniques, relevant legal developments, and advances in law enforcement equipment. Many agencies pay all or part of the tuition for officers to work toward degrees in criminal justice, police science, administration of justice, or public administration; many agencies pay higher salaries to those who earn such a degree.

Career Outlook

The opportunity for public service through law enforcement work is attractive to many because the job is challenging and involves much personal responsibility. Furthermore, law enforcement officers in many agencies may retire with a pension after twenty or twenty-five years of service, allowing them to pursue a second career while still in their forties. Because of relatively attractive salaries and benefits, the number of qualified candidates exceeds the number of job openings in federal law enforcement agencies and in most state police departments, resulting in increased hiring standards and selectivity by employers.

Competition should remain keen for higher-paying jobs with state and federal agencies and police departments in more affluent areas. Opportunities will be better in local and special police departments, especially in departments that offer relatively low salaries or in urban communities where the crime rate is relatively high. Applicants with college training in police science, military police experience, or both should have the best opportunities.

Employment of police and detectives is expected to grow faster than the average for all occupations through 2012, with a projected increase of 21 to 35 percent. A more security-conscious society and concern about drug-related crimes should contribute to the increasing demand for police services. Because the level of government spending determines employment levels for police and detectives, the number of job opportunities can vary from year to year and from place to place. On the other hand, layoffs are rare because retirements enable most staffing cuts to be handled through attrition.

Trained law enforcement officers who lose their jobs because of budget cuts usually have little difficulty finding jobs with other agencies. The need to replace workers who retire, transfer to other occupations, or stop working for other reasons will be the source of many job openings.

Salaries in Law Enforcement

Police and sheriff's patrol officers had median annual earnings of $42,270 in 2002. The middle 50 percent earned between $32,300 and $53,500. The lowest 10 percent earned less than $25,270, and the highest 10 percent earned more than $65,330. Median annual earnings were $47,090 in state government, $42,020 in local government, and $41,600 in federal government.

In 2002, median annual earnings of police and detective supervisors were $61,010. The middle 50 percent earned between $47,210 and $74,610. The lowest 10 percent earned less than $36,340, and the highest 10 percent earned more than $90,070. Median annual earnings were $78,230 in federal government, $64,410 in state government, and $59,830 in local government.

In 2002, median annual earnings of detectives and criminal investigators were $51,410. The middle 50 percent earned between $39,010 and $65,980. The lowest 10 percent earned less than $31,010, and the highest 10 percent earned more than $80,380. Median annual earnings were $66,500 in federal government, $47,700 in local government, and $46,600 in state government.

Federal law provides special salary rates to federal employees who serve in law enforcement. Additionally, federal special agents and inspectors receive law enforcement availability pay (LEAP), equal to 25 percent of the agent's grade and step, awarded because of the large amount of overtime that these agents are expected to work. For example, in 2003 FBI agents entered federal service as GS-10 employees on the pay scale at a base salary of $39,115 yet earned about $48,890 a year with availability pay. They can advance to the GS-13 grade level in field nonsupervisory assignments at a base salary of $61,251, which is worth $76,560 with availability pay.

FBI supervisory, management, and executive positions in grades GS-14 and GS-15 pay a base salary of about $72,381 or $85,140 a year, respectively, and equaled $90,480 or $106,430 per year including availability pay. Salaries were slightly higher in selected areas where the prevailing local pay level was higher. Because federal agents may be eligible for a special law enforcement benefits package, applicants should ask a recruiter for more information.

According to the International City-County Management Association's annual Police and Fire Personnel, Salaries, and Expenditures Survey, average salary ranges for sworn full-time positions in 2002 were as follows:

Police chief	$68,337–$87,037
Deputy chief	$59,790–$75,266
Police captain	$56,499–$70,177
Police lieutenant	$52,446–$63,059
Police sergeant	$46,805–$55,661
Police corporal	$39,899–$49,299

Total earnings for local, state, and special police and detectives frequently exceed the stated salary because of payments for overtime, which can be significant. In addition to the most common benefits—including paid vacation, sick leave, and medical and life insurance—most police and sheriff's departments provide officers with special allowances for uniforms. Because police officers usually are covered by liberal pension plans, many retire at half-pay after twenty or twenty-five years of service.

Correctional Officers

Although it is involved in law enforcement, the work of correctional officers differs in many ways from that of police officers, detectives, and federal agents. Correctional officers are responsible for overseeing individuals who have been arrested and are awaiting trial or who have been convicted of a crime and sentenced to serve time in a jail, reformatory, or penitentiary. They provide security and supervise inmates to prevent disturbances, assaults, or escapes. Officers have no law enforcement responsibilities outside the institution where they work.

Correctional officers maintain order within the institution and enforce rules and regulations. Officers monitor inmates' activities and supervise their work assignments. Sometimes, officers must settle disputes between inmates, enforce discipline, and search inmates and their living quarters for contraband such as weapons or drugs. Correctional officers periodically inspect the facilities, checking cells and other areas of the institution for unsanitary conditions, fire hazards, and any evidence of infractions of rules. In addition, they routinely inspect locks, window bars, grilles, doors, and gates for signs of tampering. Officers also inspect mail and visitors for prohibited items.

Correctional officers report orally and in writing on inmate conduct and on the quality and quantity of work done by inmates. Officers also report security breaches, disturbances, violations of rules, and any unusual occurrences. They usually keep a daily log or record of their activities. Correctional officers cannot show favoritism and must report any inmate who violates the rules. Should the situation arise, they help the responsible law enforcement authorities investigate crimes committed within the institution or search for escaped inmates.

In jail and prison facilities with direct-supervision cell blocks, officers work unarmed. They are equipped with communications devices so that they can summon help if necessary. These officers often work in a cell block alone or with another officer among the fifty to one hundred inmates who reside there. The officers enforce regulations primarily through their interpersonal communications skills and the use of progressive sanctions, such as loss of privileges.

In the highest-security facilities where the most dangerous inmates are housed, correctional officers often monitor the activities of prisoners from a centralized control center with the aid of closed-circuit television cameras and a computer tracking system. In such an environment, the inmates may not see anyone but officers for days or weeks at a time and only leave their cells for showers, solitary exercise time, or visitors.

Depending on the offenders' security classifications within the institution, correctional officers may have to restrain inmates in handcuffs and leg irons to safely escort them to and from cells and other areas to see authorized visitors. Officers also escort prisoners between the institution and courtrooms, medical facilities, and other destinations outside the institution.

Working Conditions

Working in a correctional institution can be stressful and hazardous. Every year, a number of correctional officers are injured in confrontations with inmates. Correctional officers may work indoors or outdoors. Some correctional institutions are well lighted, temperature controlled, and ventilated, while others are old, overcrowded, hot, and noisy.

Correctional officers usually work eight hours a day, five days a week, on rotating shifts. Prison and jail security must be provided around the clock, which often means that officers work all hours of the day and night, weekends, and holidays. In addition, officers may be required to work paid overtime.

Qualifications and Training

Most institutions require correctional officers to be United States citizens at least eighteen to twenty-one years of age; have a high school education or its equivalent; demonstrate job stability, usually by accumulating two years of work experience; and have no felony convictions. A postsecondary education may enhance prospects for promotion.

Correctional officers must be in good health. Candidates for employment are generally required to meet formal standards of physical fitness, eyesight, and hearing. Good judgment and the ability to think and act quickly are indispensable. Applicants are typically screened for drug abuse, subject to background checks, and required to pass a written examination. Many jurisdictions use standard tests to determine an applicant's suitability to work in a correctional environment.

Federal, state, and some local departments of corrections provide training for correctional officers based on guidelines established by the American Correctional Association and the American Jail Association. Some states have regional training academies that are available to local agencies. At the conclusion of formal instruction, all states and local correctional agencies provide on-the-job training, which includes instruction on legal restrictions and interpersonal relations. Many agencies and institutions require firearms proficiency and self-defense skills. Officer trainees typically receive several weeks or months of training in an actual job setting under the supervision of an experienced officer. However, specific entry requirements and on-the-job training vary widely from agency to agency.

Academy trainees generally receive instruction on a number of subjects, including institutional policies, regulations, and operations, as well as custody and security procedures. As a condition of employment, new federal correctional officers must undergo 200 hours of formal training within the first year of employment.

They also must complete 120 hours of specialized training at the U.S. Federal Bureau of Prisons residential training center at Glynco, Georgia, within the first sixty days after appointment. Experienced officers receive annual in-service training to keep abreast of new developments and procedures.

Some correctional officers are members of prison tactical response teams, which are trained to respond to disturbances, riots, hostage situations, forced cell moves, and other potentially dangerous confrontations. Team members receive training and practice with weapons, chemical agents, forced-entry methods, crisis management, and other tactics.

With education, experience, and training, qualified officers may advance to the position of correctional sergeant. Correctional sergeants supervise correctional officers and usually are responsible for maintaining security and directing the activities of other officers during an assigned shift or in an assigned area. Ambitious and qualified correctional officers can be promoted to supervisory or administrative positions all the way up to warden. Officers sometimes transfer to related positions, such as probation officer, parole officer, or correctional treatment specialist.

Job Settings

Police and sheriff's departments in county and municipal jails or precinct station houses employ many correctional officers, also known as detention officers. Most of the approximately thirty-three hundred jails in the United States are operated by county governments, with about three-quarters of all jails falling under the jurisdiction of an elected sheriff.

Most correctional officers are employed in large jails or state and federal prisons, watching over the approximately one million offenders who are incarcerated at any given time. In addition to jails and prisons, a relatively small number of correctional officers oversee individuals being held by the U.S. Immigration and

Naturalization Service before they are released or deported, or they work for correctional institutions that are run by private for-profit organizations. While both jails and prisons can be dangerous places to work, prison populations are more stable than jail populations, and officers in prisons know the security and custodial requirements of the prisoners with whom they are dealing.

Career Outlook

Job opportunities for correctional officers are expected to be excellent. The need to replace correctional officers who transfer to other occupations, retire, or leave the labor force, coupled with rising employment demand, will generate thousands of job openings each year. In the past, some local and state corrections agencies have experienced difficulty in attracting and keeping qualified applicants, largely due to relatively low salaries and the concentration of jobs in rural locations. This situation is expected to continue.

Employment of correctional officers is expected to increase from 21 to 35 percent through 2012 as additional officers are hired to supervise and control a growing inmate population. The adoption of mandatory sentencing guidelines calling for longer sentences and reduced parole for inmates will continue to spur demand for correctional officers.

Although state and local government budgetary constraints could affect the rate at which new facilities are built and staffed, expansion and new construction of corrections facilities should create many new jobs for correctional officers. Some employment opportunities will arise in the private sector as public authorities contract with private companies to provide and staff corrections facilities.

Layoffs of correctional officers are rare because of increasing offender populations. While officers are allowed to join bargaining units, they are not allowed to strike.

Salaries for Correctional Officers

Median annual earnings of correctional officers and jailers were $32,670 in 2002. The middle 50 percent earned between $25,950 and $42,620. The lowest 10 percent earned less than $22,010, and the highest 10 percent earned more than $52,370. Median annual earnings in the public sector were $40,900 in the federal government, $33,260 in state government, and $31,380 in local government. In the management and public relations industry, where the relatively small number of officers employed by privately operated prisons are classified, median annual earnings were $21,390.

According to the Federal Bureau of Prisons, the starting salary for federal correctional officers was about $23,000 a year in 2003. Starting federal salaries were slightly higher in selected areas where prevailing local pay levels were higher.

Median annual earnings of first-line supervisors and managers of correctional officers were $44,940 in 2002. The middle 50 percent earned between $33,730 and $59,160. The lowest 10 percent earned less than $29,220, and the highest 10 percent earned more than $69,370. Median annual earnings were $43,240 in state government and $49,120 in local government.

In addition to typical benefits, correctional officers employed in the public sector usually are provided with uniforms or a clothing allowance to purchase their own uniforms. Civil service systems or merit boards cover officers employed by the federal government and most state governments. Their retirement coverage entitles them to retire at age fifty after twenty years of service or at any age with twenty-five years of service.

A Close-Up Look at the Profession

Following are the personal experiences of five law enforcement professionals, from patrol officer to FBI agent. Read their accounts to see whether their careers are of interest to you.

Michael Untirdt, Patrol Officer

Michael Untirdt has been a police officer for sixteen years. He works in a village police department located near a large metropolitan city. Untirdt's interest in this career began at Western Illinois University, where he graduated with a bachelor's degree in law enforcement. He found law classes interesting and liked the idea of working outside with the public rather than behind a desk.

Untirdt was required to complete an internship during his final semester of college, and he elected to work with a police department. He says, "I felt this was very valuable because it really gave me a more realistic view of what the job entails. I was exposed to all the shifts, record keeping, radio operation—everything related to being a police officer."

Untirdt says that his daily routine might be boring to some, since "90 percent involves driving around patrolling—being on alert for individuals who are breaking the law or who look suspicious and as if they have something to hide. The rest of our time is spent responding to calls from the public and filling out reports."

The village in which Untirdt works, although becoming busier, generally sees only a few major crimes such as rape, homicide, or domestic violence. But the officers must always be ready in case such a crime occurs. As he says, "If one does [occur], and especially if it is an in-progress call, your adrenaline starts pumping and you begin to think ahead to what your course of action will be when you get close."

Untirdt stresses that certain personal qualities are important for all police officers. "Besides formal training at the academy, I believe police officers need to have common sense and the ability to relate well to all kinds of people," he explains. "This requires them to show compassion, understanding, and a healthy respect for the plight of others. I always treat everyone the way I would like to be treated."

Richard P. Saunders, Lieutenant/Patrol Commander

Lieutenant/Patrol Commander Richard P. Saunders is a member of the Tohono O'odham Nation of southern Arizona. Saunders is responsible for supervising the operations of the 172-member Tohono O'odham Nation Police Department (TOPD) in Sells, Arizona, which serves twenty-four thousand tribe members.

The TOPD is responsible for the investigation of all offenses occurring on the Tohono O'odham Nation reservation, with the exception of criminal homicides involving Native Americans, which are handled by the Federal Bureau of Investigation. Traffic and criminal violations involving Native Americans are contested in tribal court.

Felony violations involving Native Americans are contested in federal court. All violations committed by non–Native Americans, where Native American people or properties are involved, are contested in state courts.

Saunders earned an Arizona Law Enforcement Officers Advisory Council Peace Officer Certification in 1987. His background also includes one thousand hours of law-related course work and training leading to certification (criminal, traffic, tribal, state, and federal laws); Bureau of Indian Affairs Supervisory Certification, Artesia, New Mexico, 1994; and certification as a Gang Resistance Education and Training Instructor (GREAT), 1994, General Instructor Certified with an emphasis on physical fitness.

"I was recruited by a fellow tribe member working as a police officer for the Tohono O'odham Nation," Saunders says. "He told me of a very challenging and responsible career in the law enforcement profession. I saw this as an opportunity to serve my own people and work within the boundaries of my reservation while enforcing laws and protecting lives. My ability to speak the Tohono O'odham language proved to be invaluable in my daily contacts with people."

Saunders began his career in 1996 as a first-line supervisor and was soon promoted to patrol lieutenant in charge of the patrol division, recruiting staff and implementing community-oriented programs. He spent seven years as a patrol officer responding to calls for service within the Tohono O'odham Nation.

In his present position, Saunders is part of upper management. He works from ten to twelve hours a day and is on call around the clock. Saunders contributes to all decisions made regarding patrol operations and is responsible for recruiting new officers.

The Tohono O'odham Nation is comprised of 2.8 million acres located sixty miles west of Tucson. The reservation is about the same size as the state of Connecticut. The nation's eleven districts are patrolled by eighty certified police officers. The nation's lands include about sixty-three miles of the international boundary separating the Tohono O'odham, Mexico, and the United States. This boundary leads to a large number of illegal aliens and contraband coming from Mexico into the nation, adding to the duties of the police force.

Saunders describes his regular responsibilities on the job: "My daily duties include meeting with tribal elected leaders in the legislative branch to apprise them of our operations and to submit budget requests for funding, meeting with personnel in the judicial branch in order to coordinate cases and resolve detention issues, and meeting with elected leaders from the eleven political districts that comprise the Tohono O'odham Nation.

"In the case of those districts located off the main reservation, we must assist them with police protection by negotiating memorandums of understanding with neighboring non-Indian police departments, such as the Pima and Maricopa County Sheriff's Offices. I meet with tribal governmental departments, such as Health and Human Services, attorney general, prosecutors, and so forth, and with nontribal governmental agencies, such as the U.S. Border Patrol and U.S. Customs Service, to discuss ongoing issues relative to the international boundary. I receive citizens' complaints and work with our staff to resolve these matters in order to promote positive public relations with the community we serve. Due to an increase in juvenile crimes, we promote youth prevention activities and awareness to parents and school staff and administration."

In addition to these duties, Saunders attends regular meetings with supervisors to discuss departmental policies and procedures. He meets with the chief of police in management staff meetings, where departmental goals and objectives are discussed. Once a month he attends a weekend community meeting in one of the eleven districts. Here Saunders listens to public concerns and gathers input from the community while sharing the direction of the police department. It is in these meetings that his ability to speak the Tohono O'odham language is most beneficial.

On the administrative side of the job, Saunders is also responsible for payroll, including the authorization of overtime, for the entire department. In his words, "This is a very tedious and time-consuming task."

Saunders describes his general perception of the job: "The work atmosphere is stressful and intense due to the critical nature of law enforcement. What I like the most about my work is the opportunity to meet people and to learn from top administrators who have had extensive experience in this profession. This allows me to grow and develop my skills as I advance up the career ladder."

Michael A. Beltranena Jr., Director of Police

Michael A. Beltranena Jr. earned his A.A. in police administration from Rider University in Trenton, New Jersey, in 1975. He received a B.S. in police science from Rutgers University in New Brunswick, New Jersey, in 1981 and an M.A. in criminal justice from John Jay College in New York City in 1986. His additional training includes the following: New Jersey State Police Basic Municipal Police

Academy, Sea Girt, New Jersey, 1972; Nevada Highway Patrol Academy, Stead, Nevada, 1980; U.S. Secret Service Dignitary Protection Seminar, Washington, D.C., 1987; F.B.I. National Academy, Quantico, Virginia, 1989; Law Enforcement Executive Development Seminar, Quantico, Virginia, 1995. Beltranena now serves as director of police of the Montgomery Township Police Department in New Jersey.

Beltranena was attracted to the law enforcement field as a child in Brooklyn, New York, where he often visited the local police station on his way home from school. He particularly liked working with people, helping others, and the excitement of the job. His interest was further encouraged when he worked for a police director who served as Beltranena's mentor and encouraged him to set goals and to learn by observing others.

"My current job as police director is probably the most fulfilling job I have ever had," Beltranena says. "It is fun, challenging, stressful, but most important, I feel that I am able to lead a police department to provide the best possible service to the community. I work approximately sixty hours per week and enjoy every moment. Even when the stress level is high, I am still having fun and look forward to going to work."

Beltranena gains the most enjoyment from training younger officers to work ethically and professionally. "I feel that I can make a difference by developing people to take over after I am gone. The downside is when I have to deal with those who have let the agency down by not performing ethically. Another downside is having one of my officers injured. Since they are out there doing the job that I have sent them out to do, I feel responsible when they do not come back the same as when they left the station."

Aric Steven Frazier, Chairperson and Professor of Law Enforcement

Aric Steven Frazier earned an associate's degree in law enforcement at Vincennes University and bachelor's and master's degrees in science (with a major in criminal justice) at the University of Evansville in Indiana. He also holds several certifications in firearms as a master instructor through the Indiana Law Enforcement Training Board. He has served as a police officer and training officer/director at Indiana State Academy and presently is professor of law enforcement and chairperson of the law enforcement department at Vincennes University.

"First and foremost, I was drawn to this career because I enjoyed working with people," Frazier says. "I have always had an ability to keep people motivated and interested, so I feel that I am effective working in the relationship of trainer/teacher to police officers. I feel that since I enjoy this line of work so much, then others will, too.

"I always wanted to be a police officer," he says. "I know I have a facility to solve problems, and police officers need to do this on a day-to-day basis. And they will continue in this capacity because many people don't seem able to solve their problems on their own, so situations tend to recur."

While he is certainly aware of the potential dangers of police work, Frazier believes that a well-trained officer can be quite safe. As he says, "I've never felt that police work was dangerous as long as police officers use their heads and their training and education. And I feel that it is my responsibility to make others the best police they can be. I enjoy the challenge of taking charge and working together with others as a team."

Frazier loves his job and looks forward to each day's classes. His full schedule includes consulting, teaching, and serving as a college and high school basketball official at about sixty games a year. He spends his free time with his wife and children.

This is Frazier's description of a typical day: "My day starts at 5 A.M. with a good workout. I lift weights and run. From there, I lecture at least four to five hours a day, and, during office hours, I look over traffic cases sent to me by attorneys or insurance companies. If I don't have to go to the scene of an incident, I'll work it up at home instead. If going to the scene is needed, I'll go and get back home ASAP, usually about 9 P.M. to 10 P.M. (and that is true for basketball games, too)."

Kevin Illia, FBI Special Agent

Kevin Illia worked as a special agent with the FBI, serving as a recruiter in the FBI's Chicago office. Born and raised in San Francisco, he spent four years in the U.S. Air Force, two of which were in Southeast Asia during the Vietnam War. After this, he went back to school and earned his bachelor's degree from Sonoma State College in California and his master's degree in public affairs from Washington University in St. Louis.

During more than twenty-five years with the FBI, Illia served in all parts of the United States. His work included heading an antiterrorist team in San Juan, Puerto Rico. He spent more than fifteen years working out of the Chicago office.

Illia's interest in police work began during childhood. His interest in the FBI began when he served in a military police unit in the air force. As he describes it, "We had a warehouse robbery involving about a half a million dollars' worth of stolen equipment. An FBI agent assigned to the case solved it in about two hours, and I was so impressed that I decided this was the career for me. The follow-up to the story is that the agent surmised the robbery was undoubtedly an 'inside job' because the warehouse was isolated on the base. He instructed us to gather together all the personnel who worked in that warehouse (a total of ten to fifteen people) and interviewed them until he was able to elicit a confession from two or three of them. We located the stolen property the same night. Case closed."

The FBI handles more than 260 violations of federal laws, from bank robbery to crime on the high seas. This diversity is part of the job's appeal for Kevin Illia. As he says, "If you get tired of dealing with one thing, you can move to another squad that is handling an entirely different type of violation."

Illia talks about his work routine: "I'd like to describe what a typical day is like for an FBI agent, but there is no such thing. Most of the time, the plans you make are disrupted by some event that comes up unexpectedly. For instance, last Friday I was prepared to fulfill an obligation to give a presentation to some students. Then a case came up involving a fellow who had killed two individuals. Our fugitive squad was going out and needed some people, so I accompanied them. With search warrant in hand, we scoured his house and found him underneath the bathroom basin. This was a trick in itself because there are a lot of pipes under the basin and the man was six feet tall. He had his feet wrapped around the pipes somehow, as if he was a contortionist.

"The point is—you never know what your day will bring. Recently, we've had a rash of bank robberies and can be called out any time during the day to interview witnesses (or related individuals) or to appear in court to testify or appear before a grand jury.

"Another aspect of this career is that you never know where you may be called upon to travel to. A few years ago, I was working on an investigation of public corruption in Chicago and had mentioned that I'd worked in Puerto Rico. Subsequently, I got a call that they needed some people who knew the island. I was asked to leave the very next day. I thought it would be only a week, so I agreed to leave my division here in Chicago to help out down there. The week turned into two months."

Illia feels that certain skills are essential for a successful FBI agent. "You really have to be flexible and have a desire for adventure. It's also important to maintain a sense of humor, have integrity, and be a self-starter. Perseverance and tenacity are also desirable."

In addition to these qualities, Illia says that the FBI looks for individuals who are interested in making a contribution to their communities and their nation. Agents must be loyal, patriotic, and willing to make personal sacrifices. Relocation is very likely, and prospective agents must be prepared to be apart from family. As he says, "I've missed at least three Christmases and four Thanksgivings in my twenty-four year career. That can be difficult on any individual."

Kenneth Rewers, Bomb Squad Commander

Detective Kenneth Rewers is an explosives technician and bomb squad commander for the Cook County Sheriff's Police Department in Illinois.

Rewers's career began over twenty-five years ago as a patrol officer. After two years he was assigned to a task force and later moved to the detective section, where he investigated property crimes. Next he worked in homicide robbery for five years and then moved to a security detail for the state's attorney. After six years in that position, he was assigned to the bomb squad.

"Much of why I'm here today is a result of something that happened one Saturday afternoon when I was working in the detective section out of our Homewood facility," Rewers says. "Someone walked in with a pipe bomb. The desk officer told him that the detectives handle all that, so the man with the bomb walked in and laid it on my desk. I had absolutely no idea what to do, but fortunately there was one police officer on duty who had a military background and some expertise with bombs. We got him in to handle it, and that took care of that.

"Predicated on that incident and a number of others that were similar, we decided that it would be wise to set up a separate bomb unit. So I was one of the first to attend the FBI training center in Huntsville, Alabama, where all the bomb technicians in the United States and some foreign facilities are now trained. After completing a three-and-a-half-week initial training, you become certified as an explosives technician. Every fifteen to eighteen months following that, you are required to attend a one-week refresher course. In addition, our squad members train together once a week in order to share our experiences and stay on top of the most recent developments in this field."

The bomb squad in Cook County is a full-time operation, responding to more than three hundred calls a year. Members of the squad must first serve five years with the police department before applying for an explosives position. If accepted, a five-year commitment to the bomb squad is required.

As bomb squad commander, one of Rewers's duties is to recruit new members. "When we are interested in adding personnel to our explosives division, I place a notice so that those who are interested in pursuing this will get in touch with me. It is well known that our screening procedure is quite intensive and extensive. There are a number of phases in this process that candidates need to pass successfully, but the one that is foremost is the interview. Because the element of trust is so vital, all members of the squad attend to share in the decision of whether or not a candidate should be accepted."

Rewers talks about some of the situations that a bomb squad may be called on to handle: "We get a lot of pipe bomb cases, particularly associated with kids who are experimenting with various types of explosives.

"Just recently I was involved with one high school that performed a routine check of students' lockers and found an individual who had numerous books on how to build explosive devices. The local police called us. We went out there and spoke with the youth and then to his parents. The upshot of the story is that three devices were in the house already, and the parents had no idea that any of this was going on. If any of the devices had exploded, the power would have been sufficient to take the young boy's hand off."

Members of Rewers's bomb squad train with other police agencies. The squad belongs to the Great Lakes Bomb Tech Association, which includes Chicago and all the other major squads in the surrounding area. Every two months the squad has a training session in which any equipment problems are resolved and information is shared among squad members. Rewers's team also runs training sessions for local police departments to teach them proper procedures for dealing with explosives until the bomb squad arrives. They also work closely with the Bureau of Alcohol, Tobacco, and Firearms (BATF), which is the investigative agency that handles explosives cases.

"Safety is always our main concern," stresses Rewers. "You have to make the right decisions at the outset. This means that you must quickly and carefully assess the situation, confer with your partner, and decide the approach you're going to take. A mistake can bring tragic results. You may not get a second chance.

"But, even with that said, and knowing the dangers involved, we who have chosen this career find it to be both interesting and challenging."

David Jenkins, SWAT Team Member

David Jenkins, a law enforcement veteran of more than twenty years, is a member of the Northern Illinois Police Alarm System (NIPAS), a Special Weapons and Tactics (SWAT) team.

Jenkins entered the military at nineteen and served three years during the Vietnam War as a Green Beret. He worked as a light heavy-weapons specialist, training personnel behind enemy lines to engage in guerilla-type warfare.

At the end of his military service, he moved to Illinois and got a job doing security and juvenile work for School District 214. He remained in that job for three years.

In 1975 Jenkins was hired to work as a tactical officer for the police department and spent three years in the detective bureau. He also worked as a patrol officer. Jenkins has been a member of the SWAT team for the past eleven years, three on the entry team (a team of ten who are trained to go in first), about a year and a half on the marksman (or sniper) team, and since then in tactical intelligence doing background information and training for the fifty-member team.

"When SWAT teams are called in, the situations are all potentially dangerous," Jenkins says. "Otherwise they would have been handled by the local law enforcement community. Our particular SWAT team represents a unique situation in that it is a blending of team members from seventy-five towns. The group is combined in order to have a substantial team that is then at the disposal of any of the seventy-five member towns."

Anyone interested in SWAT team work must first have experience as a police officer. In Jenkins's department, candidates need at least five years of experience on patrol before applying. Individuals who are interested go through a rigorous selection process before the most desirable candidates are chosen and assigned to training. The screenings include a physical agility test and psychological tests. Those who pass the tests go into a two-week basic training period with the NIPAS team. Training continues throughout the year.

The SWAT team Jenkins works on is not a full-time operation but is called in when its expertise is required. Natural disasters, drug raids, serving high-risk warrants, hostage situations, or riots are examples of situations in which the SWAT team might be called. Team members are on call twenty-four hours a day, seven days a week. Each team member carries a pager, which the dispatch center uses to contact them in the event that they are needed.

"The SWAT service has nothing to do with working our regular shifts as police professionals in our regular assignments," Jenkins says. "If a situation comes up during a shift, I immediately grab my gear and head to the SWAT destination.

"If they need to replace me, they will send someone to take my regular assignment. If I am home, I have to have my pager on at all times. If they call me out during the night, I just respond to the incident from my home."

Jenkins talks about the realities of his work: "We've had to contend with individuals brandishing machetes, kids building bombs and threatening to blow themselves up, individuals with rifles who are threatening family members or other people. We've been called to locations where individuals have actually been in the process of shooting people and barricading themselves, sometimes with and sometimes without hostages. We never know what we'll be called up to handle.

"SWAT work is very demanding and requires a lot of sacrifice. In the eleven years I've spent on the team, I trained and handled emergencies on my own time, and it's taxing on the family sometimes. Wives and significant others sometimes have a hard time dealing with the danger, watching their loved ones being called out in the middle of the night, not knowing what's going on until the situation is resolved, one way or the other. You must really have your personal life in order because there's a lot of responsibility to this job.

"When we are able to handle a situation without firing a shot, we consider that a successful resolution. All law enforcers are interested in protecting and serving, and we want everyone to go home safe and sound. If things work out that way, we have truly fulfilled our goal."

Advice from the Professionals

Some of the professionals we have met offer good advice for anyone interested in a career in law enforcement.

Michael Untirdt shares this advice: "One way to explore an interest in this career is to look into the ride-along program that most towns offer. Try to take advantage of this opportunity by going along, particularly on differing shifts. Try to put yourself in this police officer's shoes. Ask some questions as you ride along.

Imagine yourself doing this kind of work for the next twenty or twenty-five years. Though it may be hard to project yourself so far into the future, this is a good opportunity to find out if police work is truly your calling."

Richard Saunders says: "The advice I would give to someone wanting to follow in my footsteps would be to identify a mentor with strong leadership experience. Have a dream and set both short- and long-term goals. Believe in yourself and strive toward achieving those goals. With hard work, dedication, and commitment, the goals you set for yourself will be fulfilled."

Michael Beltranena has this observation: "My advice to anyone who strives to be a police administrator is to be prepared. Continue your career, read as much as you can, adopt a mentor, and, most important, do what you know is the right thing to do."

Aric Frazier stresses the need to enjoy your work: "My advice to others would be to work hard and have fun doing it. Be sure to build a foundation by getting an education and learn as much as you can.

"Avoid easy classes and instructors. Seek out the ones that you will learn from. Be sure that this is the career for you—if not, choose another that will make you happy. Have goals and work for them and take care of yourself because no one else will."

Kevin Illia advises good preparation: "I think the more skills you bring to the FBI, the greater the opportunities for your employment. For instance, we give preference to attorneys, accountants, linguists (individuals fluent in Mandarin Chinese or Spanish, for example), individuals with scuba certification, those with private pilot licenses, paramedic certification, and/or advanced degrees.

"The more skills you have, the more valuable you are and the more competitive a candidate you will be. But you must have patience—a good deal of patience, perhaps. The process is sometimes slow and quite lengthy."

For Additional Information

Information about entrance requirements for police work may be obtained from federal, state, and local civil service commissions or police departments.

For information about police work in general, visit the website below or write to:

International Union of Police Associations
1421 Prince Street, Suite 400
Alexandria, VA 22314
www.iupa.org

Links to all U.S. federal agencies are available at the White House website. Select the link for Agencies and Commissions at www.whitehouse.gov/government.

Another website that provides access to all branches of the federal government is www.first.gov.

Information about entrance requirements, training, and career opportunities for correctional officers at the state level may be obtained from your state's civil service commission, department of correction, or directly from individual correctional institutions in your area. Or contact:

The American Jail Association
1135 Professional Court
Hagerstown, MD 21740
www.corrections.com/aja

Information on entrance requirements, training, and career opportunities for correctional officers at the federal level may be obtained from:

Federal Bureau of Prisons
National Recruitment Office
320 First Street NW, Room 460
Washington, DC 20534
www.bop.gov

The following website provides information on various types of correctional facilities, as well as links to associations and educational information: www.corrections.com.

CHAPTER THREE

Careers in Firefighting and Emergency Medical Services

I think patriotism is like charity—it begins at home.
—Henry James

The first fire departments consisted of neighbors who got together in times of crisis to help one another. "Bucket brigades" were formed to connect the closest sources of water to the fire, with volunteers working together to help one another. By the turn of the century, most local municipalities began to establish their own professional fire departments as well as medical emergency response services, which may be a separate agency or part of the fire department.

Firefighters

Every year, fires and other emergencies take thousands of lives and destroy property worth billions of dollars. Firefighters help to protect the public against these dangers by rapidly responding to a variety of emergencies. They are frequently the first emergency personnel at the scene of a medical emergency or traffic accident, where they may be called upon to put out a fire, treat injuries, or perform other vital functions.

While on duty, firefighters must be prepared to respond immediately to a fire or any other emergency that arises. Because of the dangerous and complex nature of fighting fires, the work requires organization and teamwork. At every emergency scene, firefighters perform specific duties assigned by a superior officer. At fires, they connect hose lines to hydrants, operate a pump to send water to high-pressure hoses, and position ladders to enable them to deliver water to the fire. They also rescue victims and provide emergency medical attention as needed, ventilate smoke-filled areas, and attempt to salvage the contents of buildings. Their duties may change several times while the company is in action. Sometimes they remain at the site of a disaster for days at a time, rescuing trapped survivors and assisting with medical treatment.

The work of firefighters includes a broad range of responsibilities, including emergency medical services. In fact, most calls to which firefighters respond involve medical emergencies, and about half of all fire departments provide ambulance service for victims. Firefighters receive training in emergency medical procedures, and many fire departments require them to be certified as emergency medical technicians.

Between alarms, firefighters clean and maintain equipment, conduct practice drills and fire inspections, and participate in physical fitness activities. They also prepare written reports on fire incidents and review fire science literature to keep abreast of technological developments and changing administrative practices and policies.

Most fire departments have a fire prevention division, usually headed by a fire marshall and staffed by fire inspectors. Workers in this division conduct inspections of structures to prevent fires and ensure compliance with fire codes. These firefighters also work with developers and planners to check and approve plans for new buildings. Fire prevention personnel often speak about fire prevention in schools and before public assemblies and for civic organizations.

Some firefighters become fire investigators, working to determine the origins and causes of fires. They collect evidence, interview witnesses, and prepare reports on fires in cases where the cause may be arson or criminal negligence. They often are called upon to testify in court.

Working Conditions

Firefighters spend much of their time at fire stations, which usually have accommodations for eating and sleeping. The members of a fire company often take turns preparing meals in the station kitchen. When an alarm sounds, firefighters respond rapidly, regardless of the weather or hour.

Firefighting involves risk of death or injury from sudden cave-ins of floors, toppling walls, traffic accidents when responding to calls, and exposure to flames and smoke. Firefighters may also come into contact with poisonous, flammable, or explosive gases and chemicals, as well as radioactive or other hazardous materials that may have immediate or long-term effects on their health. For these reasons, they must wear protective gear that can be very heavy and hot.

Firefighters often work long and varied shifts. Many work fifty hours a week, and sometimes they may work even longer. In some agencies, they are on duty for twenty-four hours, then off for forty-eight hours, and they receive an extra day off at intervals. In others, they work a day shift of ten hours for three or four days, a night shift of fourteen hours for three or four nights, have three or four days off, and then repeat the cycle. In addition, firefighters often work extra hours at fires and other emergencies and are regularly assigned to work on holidays. Fire lieutenants and fire captains often work the same hours as the firefighters they supervise.

Duty hours include time when firefighters study, train, and perform fire prevention duties.

Qualifications and Training

Applicants for municipal firefighting jobs generally must pass a written exam; tests of strength, physical stamina, coordination, and agility; and a medical examination that includes drug screening. (Once hired, workers may be monitored for drug use on a random basis.) Examinations are generally open to candidates who are at least eighteen years of age and have a high school education or the equivalent. Those who receive the highest scores in all phases of testing have the best chances for appointment, and completion of community college courses in fire science may improve an applicant's standing. In recent years, an increasing proportion of firefighting recruits have had some postsecondary education.

As a rule, entry-level workers in large fire departments are trained for several weeks at the department's training center or academy. Through classroom instruction and practical training, the recruits study firefighting techniques, fire prevention, hazardous materials control, local building codes, and emergency medical procedures, including first aid and cardiopulmonary resuscitation. They also learn how to use axes, chain saws, fire extinguishers, ladders, and other firefighting and rescue equipment. After they have successfully completed this training, they are assigned to a fire company, where they undergo a period of probation.

A number of fire departments have accredited apprenticeship programs lasting up to five years. These programs combine formal, technical instruction with on-the-job training under the supervision of experienced firefighters. Technical instruction covers subjects such as firefighting techniques and equipment, chemical hazards associated with various combustible building materials, emergency medical procedures, and fire prevention and safety.

Fire departments frequently conduct training programs, and some firefighters attend training sessions sponsored by the National Fire Academy. These training sessions cover topics including executive development, anti-arson techniques, disaster preparedness, hazardous materials control, and public fire safety and education. Some states also have extensive firefighter training and certification programs. In addition, a number of colleges and universities offer courses leading to two- or four-year degrees in fire engineering or fire science. Many fire departments offer firefighters incentives, such as tuition reimbursement or higher pay, for completing advanced training.

Among the personal qualities needed by firefighters are mental alertness, self-discipline, courage, mechanical aptitude, endurance, strength, and a sense of public service. Initiative and good judgment are also extremely important because firefighters must make quick decisions in emergencies. Because members of a crew live and work closely together under conditions of stress and danger for extended periods, they must be dependable and able to get along well with others. Leadership qualities are necessary for officers, who must establish and maintain discipline and efficiency, as well as direct the activities of firefighters in their companies.

Most experienced firefighters continue studying to improve their job performance and prepare for promotion examinations. To progress to higher-level positions, they acquire expertise in advanced firefighting equipment and techniques, building construction, emergency medical technology, writing, public speaking, management and budgeting procedures, and public relations.

Opportunities for promotion depend on written examination results, job performance, interviews, and seniority. Increasingly, fire departments use assessment centers, which simulate a variety of actual job performance tasks, to screen for the best candidates for promotion. The line of promotion usually is to engineer, lieutenant, captain, battalion chief, assistant chief, deputy chief, and finally to chief. Many fire departments now require a bachelor's degree, preferably in fire science, public administration, or a related field, for promotion to positions higher than battalion chief. A master's degree is required for executive fire officer certification from the National Fire Academy and for state chief officer certification.

Job Settings

Firefighters work in a variety of settings, including urban and suburban areas, airports, chemical plants, other industrial sites, and rural areas, such as grasslands and forests. In addition, some firefighters work in hazardous materials units that are specially trained for the control, prevention, and cleanup of oil spills and other hazardous materials incidents. Workers in urban and suburban areas, airports, and industrial sites typically use conventional firefighting equipment and tactics, while forest fires and major hazardous materials spills call for different methods.

In national forests and parks, forest fire inspectors and prevention specialists spot fires from watchtowers and report their findings to headquarters by telephone or radio. Forest rangers patrol to ensure that travelers and campers comply with fire regulations. When fires break out, crews of firefighters are brought in to suppress the blaze using heavy equipment, hand tools, and water hoses.

Forest firefighting, like urban firefighting, can be rigorous work. One of the most effective means of battling these blazes is by creating fire lines: cutting down trees and digging out grass and all other combustible vegetation to create bare land in the path of the fire, which deprives it of fuel. Elite firefighters, called smoke jumpers, parachute from airplanes to reach otherwise inaccessible areas. This can be extremely hazardous because the crews have no way to escape if the wind shifts and causes the fire to burn toward them.

According the U.S. Fire Administration, nearly 70 percent of fire companies are staffed by volunteer firefighters. Volunteer firefighters perform the same duties as their paid counterparts and often comprise the majority of firefighters in rural areas.

About nine out of ten firefighting workers are employed by municipal or county fire departments. Some large cities have thousands of career firefighters, while many small towns have only a few. Most of the remainder work in fire departments on federal and state installations, including airports. Private firefighting companies employ a small number of firefighters and usually operate on a subscription basis.

In response to the expanding role of firefighters, some municipalities have combined fire prevention, public fire education, safety, and emergency medical services into a single organization commonly referred to as a public safety organization. Some local and regional fire departments are being consolidated into countywide establishments in order to reduce administrative staffs and cut costs and to establish consistent training standards and work procedures.

Career Outlook

Strong competition is expected for paid firefighting positions. Many people are attracted to a career in firefighting because it is challenging and provides the opportunity to perform an essential public service.

In addition, a high school education is usually sufficient for entry, and a pension is guaranteed upon retirement after twenty years. Consequently, the number of qualified applicants in most areas exceeds the number of job openings, even though the written examination and physical requirements eliminate many applicants. This situation is expected to persist in coming years.

Employment of firefighters is expected to grow about as fast as the average for all occupations through 2012 (between 10 and 20 percent) as fire departments continue to compete with other public safety providers for funding.

Most job growth will occur as volunteer firefighting positions are converted to paid positions. In addition to job growth, openings are expected to result from the need to replace firefighters who retire, stop working for other reasons, or transfer to other occupations.

Layoffs of firefighters are uncommon. Fire protection is an essential service, and citizens are likely to exert considerable pressure on local officials to expand or at least preserve the level of fire protection. Even when budget cuts do occur, local fire departments usually cut expenses by postponing equipment purchases or not hiring new firefighters rather than through staff reductions.

Salaries for Firefighters

Median hourly earnings of firefighters were $17.42 in 2002. The middle 50 percent earned between $12.53 and $22.96. The lowest 10 percent earned less than $8.51, and the highest 10 percent earned more than $28.22. Median hourly earnings were $17.92 in local government, $15.96 in the federal government, and $13.58 in state government.

Median annual earnings of first-line supervisors and managers of firefighting and prevention workers were $55,450 in 2002. The middle 50 percent earned between $43,920 and $68,480. The lowest 10 percent earned less than $34,190, and the highest 10 percent earned more than $84,730. First-line supervisors and managers of firefighting and prevention workers employed in local government earned about $56,390 a year in 2002.

Median annual earnings of fire inspectors were $44,250 in 2002. The middle 50 percent earned between $33,880 and $56,100 a year. The lowest 10 percent earned less than $26,350, and the highest 10 percent earned more than $69,060.

Fire inspectors and investigators employed in local government earned about $46,820 a year. According to the International City-County Management Association, average salary ranges in 2002 for sworn full-time positions were as follows:

Fire chief	$64,134–$82,225
Deputy chief	$56,522–$72,152
Assistant fire chief	$55,645–$69,036
Battalion chief	$54,935–$68,673
Fire captain	$45,383–$54,463
Fire lieutenant	$41,800–$49,404
Fire prevention/code inspector	$40,387–$51,531
Engineer	$38,656–$48,678

Firefighters who average more than a certain number of hours a week are required to be paid overtime. The hours threshold is determined by the department during the firefighter's work period, which ranges from seven to twenty-eight days. Firefighters often earn overtime for working extra shifts to maintain minimum staffing levels or for special emergencies.

Firefighters receive benefits that usually include medical and liability insurance, vacation and sick leave, and some paid holidays. Almost all fire departments provide protective clothing (helmets, boots, and coats) and breathing apparatuses, and many also provide dress uniforms. Firefighters are generally covered by pension plans, often providing retirement at half pay after twenty-five years of service or if disabled in the line of duty.

Emergency Medical Technicians and Paramedics

In some municipalities, emergency response services are provided by firefighters, who also work as emergency medical technicians or paramedics. In other areas, firefighting and emergency response services are separate professions.

People's lives often depend on the quick reactions and competent care of emergency medical technicians (EMTs) and paramedics, who are EMTs with additional advanced training that enables them to perform more difficult out-of-hospital medical procedures. Incidents such as automobile accidents, heart attacks, drownings, childbirth, and gunshot wounds all require immediate medical attention. EMTs and paramedics provide this vital attention as they care for and transport the sick or injured to a medical facility.

In an emergency, EMTs and paramedics typically are dispatched to the scene by a 911 operator and often work with police and fire department personnel. Once they arrive at the scene, EMTs determine the nature and extent of the patient's condition while trying to ascertain whether the patient has preexisting medical problems. Following strict rules and guidelines, they give appropriate emergency care and, when necessary, transport the patient. Some paramedics are trained to treat patients with minor injuries at the scene of an accident or at their home without transporting them to a medical facility. Emergency treatment for more complicated problems is carried out under the direction of medical doctors by radio preceding or during transport.

EMTs and paramedics may use special equipment, such as backboards, to immobilize patients before placing them on stretchers and securing them in the ambulance for transport to a medical facility. Usually, one EMT or paramedic drives while the other monitors the patient's vital signs and gives additional care as needed. Some EMTs work as part of the flight crew of helicopters that transport critically ill or injured patients to hospital trauma centers.

At the medical facility, EMTs and paramedics help transfer patients to the emergency department, report their observations and actions to emergency room staff, and may provide additional emergency treatment. After each run, EMTs and paramedics replace used supplies and check equipment. If a transported patient had a contagious disease, the workers must decontaminate the interior of the ambulance and report such cases to the proper health authorities.

Beyond these general duties, the specific responsibilities of EMTs and paramedics depend on their level of qualification and training. The National Registry of Emergency Medical Technicians (NREMT) registers emergency medical service providers at four levels: First Responder, EMT-Basic, EMT-Intermediate, and EMT-Paramedic. Some states, however, do their own certifications and use numeric ratings from one to four to distinguish levels of proficiency.

First Responders, the lowest-level workers, are trained to provide basic emergency medical care because they are usually the first to arrive at the scene of an incident. Many firefighters, police officers, and other emergency workers have this level of training. The EMT-Basic, also known as EMT-1, represents the first component of the emergency medical technician system. An EMT-1 is trained to care for patients at the scene of an accident and while transporting patients by ambulance to the hospital under medical direction. The EMT-1 has the skills to assess a patient's condition and manage respiratory, cardiac, and trauma emergencies.

The EMT-Intermediate (EMT-2 and EMT-3) has more advanced training that allows the administration of intravenous fluids, the use of manual defibrillators to give lifesaving shocks to a stopped heart, and the application of advanced airway techniques and equipment to assist patients experiencing respiratory emergencies.

EMT-Paramedics (EMT-4s) provide the most extensive prehospital care. In addition to carrying out the procedures already described for other levels, paramedics may administer drugs both orally and intravenously, interpret electrocardiograms (EKGs) and monitor readouts, perform endotracheal intubations, and use other complex equipment.

Working Conditions

EMTs and paramedics work both indoors and outdoors in all types of weather. Their work generally requires considerable kneeling, bending, and heavy lifting. These workers risk noise-induced hearing loss from sirens and back injuries from lifting patients. In addition, EMTs and paramedics may be exposed to diseases such as hepatitis-B and AIDS, as well as violence from drug overdose victims or mentally unstable patients. The work is not only physically strenuous, but also stressful, involving life-or-death situations and suffering patients. Nonetheless, many people find the work exciting and challenging and enjoy the opportunity to help others.

EMTs and paramedics employed by fire departments work about fifty hours a week. Those employed by hospitals frequently work between forty-five and sixty hours a week, and those in private ambulance services work between forty-five and fifty hours. Some of these workers, especially those in police and fire departments, are on call for extended periods. Because emergency services function twenty-four hours a day, EMTs and paramedics have irregular working hours, which can add to job stress.

Qualifications and Training

Formal training and certification are needed to become an EMT or paramedic. All fifty states have a certification procedure. In most states and the District of Columbia, registration with the NREMT is required at some or all levels of certification. Other states administer their own certification examinations or provide the option of taking the NREMT examination.

To maintain certification, EMTs and paramedics must reregister, usually every two years. In order to reregister, an individual must be working as an EMT or a paramedic and meet the continuing education requirement.

Training is offered at three progressive levels: EMT-Basic, EMT-Intermediate, and EMT-Paramedic. EMT-Basic course work typically emphasizes patient assessment and emergency skills, such as managing respiratory, trauma, and cardiac emergencies.

Formal courses are often combined with time spent working in an emergency room or ambulance. The program also provides instruction and practice in dealing with bleeding, fractures, airway obstruction, cardiac arrest, and emergency childbirth. Students learn how to use and maintain common emergency equipment, such as suction devices, splints, oxygen-delivery systems, backboards, and stretchers.

Graduates of approved EMT-Basic training programs who pass both written and practical examinations administered by the state certifying agency or the NREMT earn the title Registered EMT-Basic. The training course also is oone of the prerequisites for EMT-Intermediate and EMT-Paramedic training.

Training requirements for EMT-Intermediate certification are different from state to state. Applicants can choose to receive training in EMT-Shock Trauma, which involves learning to start intravenous fluids and to give certain medications, or in EMT-Cardiac, which includes learning heart rhythms and administering advanced medications.

Training commonly includes thirty-five to fifty-five hours of additional instruction beyond EMT-Basic course work and covers patient assessment as well as the use of advanced airway devices and intravenous fluids. The prerequisites for taking the EMT-Intermediate examination include registration as an EMT-Basic, completion of required classroom work, and a specified amount of clinical experience.

The most advanced level of training is EMT-Paramedic. At this level, the caregiver receives additional training in body function and learns more advanced skills. The technology program usually lasts up to two years and results in an associate's degree in applied science. This prepares the graduate to take the NREMT examination and become certified as an EMT-Paramedic. Extensive related course work and clinical and field experience are required. Due to the longer training requirement, almost all EMT-Paramedics are in paid positions, rather than working as volunteers. Refresher courses and continuing education are available for EMTs and paramedics at all levels.

EMTs and paramedics should be emotionally stable; have good dexterity, agility, and physical coordination; and be able to lift and carry heavy loads. They also need good eyesight (corrective lenses may be used) with accurate color vision.

Advancement beyond the EMT-Paramedic level usually means leaving fieldwork. An EMT-Paramedic can become a supervisor, operations manager, administrative director, or executive director of emergency services. Some EMTs and paramedics become instructors, dispatchers, or physician assistants, while others move into sales or marketing of emergency medical equipment. A number of people become EMTs and paramedics to assess their interest in health care; some of them decide to return to school and become registered nurses, physicians, or other health workers.

Career Outlook

Employment of emergency medical technicians and paramedics is expected to grow faster than the average for all occupations through 2012, between 21 and 35 percent. Population growth and urbanization will increase the demand for full-time paid EMTs and paramedics rather than for volunteers.

In addition, a large segment of the population—the aging baby boomers—will further spur demand for EMT services as they become more likely to have medical emergencies. There will still be demand for part-time and volunteer EMTs and paramedics in rural areas and smaller metropolitan areas.

In addition to those arising from job growth, openings will occur because of replacement needs; some workers leave the occupation because of stressful working conditions, limited potential for advancement, and the modest pay and benefits in private-sector jobs.

Most opportunities for EMTs and paramedics are expected to be found in private ambulance services. Competition will be greater for jobs in local government, including fire, police, and independent third-service rescue squad departments, in which salaries and benefits tend to be slightly better.

Opportunities will be best for those who have advanced certifications, such as EMT-Intermediate and EMT-Paramedic, as clients and patients demand higher levels of care before arriving at the hospital.

Salaries for EMTs and Paramedics

Earnings of EMTs and paramedics depend on the employment setting and geographic location as well as the individual's training and experience. Median annual earnings of EMTs and paramedics were $24,030 in 2002.

The middle 50 percent earned between $19,040 and $31,600. The lowest 10 percent earned less than $15,530, and the highest 10 percent earned more than $41,980. Median annual earnings in the industries employing the largest numbers of EMTs and paramedics in 2002 were:

Local government	$27,440
General medical and surgical hospitals	$24,760
Other ambulatory health care services	$22,180

Those in emergency medical services who are part of fire or police departments receive the same benefits as firefighters or police officers. For example, many are covered by pension plans that provide retirement at half pay after twenty or twenty-five years of service or if the worker is disabled in the line of duty.

For Additional Information

The following professional associations offer information about education and training requirements as well as a variety of career opportunities.

Firefighters

Canadian Association of Fire Chiefs
PO Box 1227
Station B
Ottawa, ON K1P 5R3
Canada
www.cafc.ca

International Association of Fire Chiefs
4025 Fair Ridge Drive
Fairfax, VA 22033
www.iafc.org

International Association of Fire Fighters
1750 New York Avenue NW
Washington, DC 20006
www.iaff.org

National Fire Protection Association
One Batterymarch Park
Quincy, MA 02169
www.nfpa.org

U.S. Fire Administration and National Fire Academy
16825 South Seaton Avenue
Emmitsburg, MD 21727
www.usfa.fema.gov

Emergency Medical Technicians and Paramedics

International Association of EMTs and Paramedics
159 Burgin Parkway
Quincy, MA 02169
www.iaep.org

National Registry of Emergency Medical Technicians
PO Box 29233
Columbus, OH 43229
www.nremt.org

Paramedic Association of Canada
300 March Road, Fourth Floor
Ottawa, ON K2K 2E2
Canada
www.paramedic.ca

CHAPTER FOUR

Careers in the Military

I only regret that I have but one life to lose for my country.
—Nathan Hale

For many, the desire to serve one's country and see the world is best fulfilled by spending time in the military. And fortunately this is the case, because a strong national defense depends on a vast number of individuals performing diverse jobs. These include (among others) managing hospitals, commanding tank crews, programming computers, operating nuclear reactors, and repairing and maintaining helicopters. The military's occupational diversity provides educational opportunities and work experience in literally hundreds of jobs for those willing to make the commitment to their country.

The Military Branches

The United States military is divided into five main branches that each play a specific role in our national defense.

- **Air Force, Air Force Reserve, and Air National Guard.** The air force branches defend the United States by controlling air and space. Stationed all over the world, they fly and maintain aircraft, missiles, and spacecraft.

- **Army, Army Reserve, and Army National Guard.** These forces protect and defend the United States and its interests by maintaining ground troops, tanks, helicopters, and missile systems. They may be involved in land-based operations all over the world.
- **Coast Guard and Coast Guard Reserve.** These forces serve as a branch of the armed services and as a service within the U.S. Department of Transportation. They act as the main maritime law enforcement agency for the United States.
- **Navy and Navy Reserve.** Naval forces defend the United States and its allies, providing clear access to travel throughout the world's oceans. Navy personnel may serve on submarines, on ships, at bases on shore, and in aviation positions in any part of the world.
- **Marine Corps and Marine Corps Reserve.** Marine troops combine to form an elite fighting force that operates within the Department of the Navy. Marines guard United States embassies, protect naval bases, serve on ships, and remain ready at a moment's notice to protect the interests of the United States anywhere in the world.

Military Personnel

The military distinguishes between enlisted and officer careers. Enlisted personnel, who make up about 85 percent of the armed forces, carry out the fundamental operations of the military in areas such as combat, administration, construction, engineering, health care, and human services. Officers make up the remaining 15 percent of the armed forces and are the leaders of the military, supervising and managing activities in every occupational specialty of the military.

Careers for Enlisted Personnel

Administrative Careers. The military must maintain accurate information for planning and managing its operations; therefore, administrative careers include a wide variety of positions. Both paper and electronic records are kept on personnel and on equipment, funds, supplies, and other property of the military. Enlisted administrative personnel record information, type reports, maintain files, and review information to assist military officers.

Personnel may work in a specialized area, such as finance, accounting, legal affairs, maintenance, supply, or transportation. Some examples of administrative specialists are recruiting specialists, who recruit and place qualified personnel and provide information about military careers to young people, parents, schools, and local communities; training specialists and instructors, who provide the training programs necessary to help people perform their jobs effectively; and personnel specialists, who collect and store information about individuals in the military, including information on their training, job assignments, promotions, and health.

Combat Specialty Occupations. These positions refer to enlisted specialties, such as infantry, artillery, and special forces, whose members operate weapons or execute special missions during combat. Persons in these occupations normally specialize by the type of weapon system or combat operation. These personnel maneuver against enemy forces and position and fire artillery, guns, and missiles to destroy enemy positions. They also may operate tanks and amphibious assault vehicles in combat or on scouting missions.

When the military has difficult and dangerous missions to perform, it calls upon special-operations teams. These elite combat forces maintain a constant state of readiness to strike anywhere in the world on a moment's notice. Team members from the special-operations forces conduct offensive raids, demolitions, intelligence, search-and-rescue missions, and other operations from aboard aircraft, helicopters, ships, or submarines.

Construction Occupations. In the military, construction involves personnel who build or repair buildings, airfields, bridges, foundations, dams, bunkers, and all the electrical and plumbing components of these structures. Enlisted personnel in construction occupations operate bulldozers, cranes, graders, and other heavy equipment. Construction specialists also may work with engineers and other building specialists as part of military construction teams. Some personnel specialize in areas such as plumbing or electrical wiring. Plumbers and pipe fitters install and repair the plumbing and pipe systems needed in buildings and on aircraft and ships. Building electricians install and repair electrical wiring systems in offices, airplane hangars, and other buildings on military bases.

Electronic and Electrical Equipment Repair Personnel. These workers repair and maintain electronic and electrical equipment used in the military. Repairers normally specialize by type of equipment, such as avionics, computer, optical, communications, or weapons systems. For example, electronic instrument repairers install, test, maintain, and repair a wide variety of electronic systems, including navigational controls and biomedical instruments. Weapons maintenance technicians maintain and repair weapons used by combat forces; most of these weapons have electronic components and systems that assist in locating targets and in aiming and firing the weapons.

Engineering, Science, and Technical Occupations. The military has many occupations in these areas, requiring workers with specific knowledge to operate technical equipment, solve complex problems, or provide and interpret information. Enlisted personnel normally specialize in one area, such as space operations, emergency management, environmental health and safety, or intelligence. Space operations specialists use and repair ground-control command equipment having to do with spacecraft, including electronic systems that track the location and operation of a craft. Emergency management specialists prepare emergency procedures for all types of disasters, such as floods, tornadoes, and earthquakes. Environmental health and safety specialists inspect military facilities and food supplies for the presence of disease, germs, or other conditions hazardous to health and the environment. Intelligence specialists gather and study information by means of aerial photographs and various types of radar and surveillance systems.

Health Care Personnel. These workers assist medical professionals in treating and providing services for men and women in the military. They may work as part of a patient-service team in close contact with doctors, dentists, nurses, and physical therapists to provide the necessary support functions within a hospital or clinic. Health care specialists normally specialize in a particular area, such as emergency medical treatment, the operation of diagnostic tools such as x-ray and ultrasound equipment, laboratory testing of tissue and blood samples, or maintaining pharmacy supplies or patients' records, among others.

Human Resources Development Specialists. These specialists recruit and place qualified personnel and provide the training programs necessary to help people perform their jobs effectively. Personnel in this career area normally specialize by activity. For example, recruiting specialists provide information about military careers to young people, parents, schools, and local communities and explain the armed service's employment and training opportunities, pay and benefits, and service life.

Personnel specialists collect and store information about the people in the military, including information on their previous and current training, job assignments, promotions, and health. Training specialists and instructors teach classes and give demonstrations to provide military personnel with the knowledge they need to perform their jobs.

Machine Operation and Production Occupations. Armed forces personnel in these positions operate industrial equipment, machinery, and tools to fabricate and repair parts for a variety of items and structures. They may operate engines, turbines, nuclear reactors, and water pumps. Often, they specialize by the type of work performed. Welders and metalworkers, for instance, work with various types of metals to repair or form the structural parts of ships, submarines, buildings, or other equipment. Survival equipment specialists inspect, maintain, and repair survival equipment, such as parachutes and aircraft life-support equipment. Dental and optical laboratory technicians construct and repair dental equipment and eyeglasses for military personnel.

Media and Public Affairs Occupations. These specialties deal with the public presentation and interpretation of military information and events. Enlisted media and public affairs personnel take and develop photographs; film, record, and edit video and audio programs; present news and music programs; and produce graphic artwork, drawings, and other visual displays. Still other public affairs specialists work as interpreters and translators.

Protective Service Personnel. Those who enforce military laws and regulations, provide emergency response to natural and human-made disasters, and maintain food standards fall into this category. These personnel normally specialize by function. For example, military police control traffic, prevent crime, and respond to emergencies. Other law enforcement and security specialists investigate crimes committed on military property and guard inmates in military correctional facilities. Firefighters put out, control, and help prevent fires in buildings, on aircraft, and aboard ships. Food-service specialists prepare all types of food in dining halls, hospitals, and ships.

Transportation and Material Handling Specialists. The main responsibility of workers in this occupation is to ensure the safe transport of people and cargo. Most personnel within this group are classified according to mode of transportation, such as aircraft, motor vehicle, or ship. The air crew operates equipment on board aircraft during operations. Vehicle drivers operate all types of heavy military vehicles, including fuel or water tank trucks, semitrailers, heavy troop transports, and passenger buses. Quartermasters and boat operators navigate and pilot many types of small watercraft, including tugboats, gunboats, and barges. Cargo specialists load and unload military supplies, using equipment such as forklifts and cranes.

Vehicle and Machinery Mechanics. These mechanics conduct preventive and corrective maintenance on aircraft, ships, automotive and heavy equipment, heating and cooling systems, marine engines, and powerhouse station equipment. They typically specialize by the type of equipment that they maintain. For example, aircraft mechanics inspect, service, and repair helicopters and airplanes. Automotive and heavy-equipment mechanics maintain and repair jeeps, cars, trucks, tanks, self-propelled missile launchers, and other combat vehicles. They also repair bulldozers, power shovels, and other construction equipment.

Heating and cooling mechanics install and repair heating equipment, air-conditioning, and refrigeration units. Marine engine mechanics repair and maintain gasoline and diesel engines on ships, boats, and other watercraft. They also repair shipboard mechanical and electrical equipment. Powerhouse mechanics install, maintain, and repair electrical and mechanical equipment in power-generating stations.

Careers for Military Officers

Combat Specialty Officers. These officers plan and direct military operations, oversee combat activities, and serve as combat leaders. This category includes officers in charge of tanks and other armored assault vehicles, artillery systems, special operations forces, and infantry. Combat specialty officers normally specialize by the type of unit that they lead. Within the unit, they may specialize by the type of weapon system. Artillery and missile system officers, for example, direct personnel as they target, launch, test, and maintain various types of missiles and artillery. Special-operations officers lead their units in offensive raids, demolitions, intelligence gathering, and search-and-rescue missions.

Engineering, Science, and Technical Officers. Officers in this category have a wide range of responsibilities based on their area of expertise. They lead or perform activities in areas such as space operations, environmental health and safety, and engineering. These officers may direct the operations of communications centers or the development of complex computer systems. Environmental health and safety officers study the air, ground, and water to identify and analyze the sources and effects of pollution. They also direct programs to control safety and health hazards in the workplace. Other personnel work as aerospace engineers to design and direct the development of military aircraft, missiles, and spacecraft.

Executive, Administrative, and Managerial Officers. These officers oversee and direct military activities in key functional areas, such as finance, accounting, health administration, international relations, and supply. Health services administrators, for instance, are responsible for the overall quality of care provided at the hospitals and clinics they operate. They must ensure that each department works together to provide the highest quality of care. Another example is purchasing and contracting managers, who negotiate and monitor contracts for the purchase of the billions of dollars worth of equipment, supplies, and services that the military buys from private industry each year.

Health Care Officers. Health services at military facilities are provided by health care officers on the basis of their area of specialization. Officers who assist in examining, diagnosing, and treating patients suffering from illness, injury, or disease include physicians, registered nurses, and dentists. Other health care officers provide therapy, rehabilitative treatment, and additional services for patients. Physical and occupational therapists plan and administer therapy to help patients adjust to disabilities, regain independence, and return to work. Speech therapists evaluate and treat patients with hearing and speech problems. Dietitians manage food service facilities and plan meals for hospital patients and for outpatients who need special diets. Pharmacists manage the purchase, storage, and dispensation of drugs and medicines. Physicians and surgeons in this occupational group provide the majority of medical services to the military and their families. Dentists treat diseases and disorders of the mouth. Optometrists treat vision problems by prescribing eyeglasses or contact lenses. Psychologists provide mental health care and also conduct research on behavior and emotions.

Media and Public Affairs Officers. These officers oversee the development, production, and presentation of information or events for the public. They may produce and direct motion pictures, videotapes, and television and radio broadcasts that are used for training, news, and entertainment. Some plan, develop, and direct the activities of military bands. Public information officers respond to inquiries about military activities and prepare news releases and reports to keep the public informed.

Protective Service Officers. The responsibility for the safety and protection of individuals and property on military bases and vessels falls to protective service officers. Emergency management officers plan and prepare for all types of natural and human-made disasters. They develop warning, control, and evacuation plans to be used in the event of a disaster. Law enforcement and security officers enforce all applicable laws on military bases and investigate crimes when the law has been broken.

Support Service Officers. Officers in this occupational group manage food service activities and perform services in support of the morale and well-being of military personnel and their families. Food service managers oversee the preparation and delivery of food services within dining facilities located on military installations and vessels. Social workers focus on improving conditions that can cause social problems, such as drug and alcohol abuse, racism, and sexism. Chaplains conduct worship services for military personnel and perform other spiritual duties covering the beliefs and practices of all religious faiths.

Transportation Occupations. Officers in transportation occupations manage and perform activities related to the safe transport of military personnel and material by air and water. Officers normally specialize by mode of transportation or area of expertise because in many cases they must meet licensing and certification requirements. Pilots in the military fly various types of specialized airplanes and helicopters to carry troops and equipment and to execute combat missions. Navigators use radar, radio, and other navigation equipment to determine their positions and plan their travel routes. Officers on ships and submarines work as a team to manage the various departments aboard their vessels. Ships' engineers direct engineering departments aboard ships and submarines, including engine operations, maintenance, repair, heating, and power generation.

Warrant Officers. Warrant officers are technical and tactical leaders who specialize in a specific technical area; for example, army aviators make up one group of warrant officers. The Army Warrant Officer Corps constitutes less than 5 percent of the total army. Although the corps is small in size, its level of responsibility is high. Its members receive extended career opportunities, worldwide leadership assignments, and increased pay and retirement benefits. Selection to attend the Warrant Officer Candidate School is highly competitive and restricted to those with the rank of E-5 or higher.

Qualifications and Training

Enlisted Personnel. In order to join the services, enlisted personnel must sign a legal agreement called an enlistment contract, which usually involves a commitment to eight years of service. Depending on the terms of the contract, two to six years are spent on active duty, and the balance is spent in the reserves. The enlistment contract obligates the service to provide the agreed-upon job, rating, pay, cash bonuses for enlistment in certain occupations, medical and other benefits, occupational training, and continuing education. In return, enlisted personnel must serve satisfactorily for the period specified.

Requirements for each service vary, but certain qualifications for enlistment are common to all branches. In order to enlist, one must be between seventeen and thirty-five years old, be a United States citizen or an alien holding permanent resident status, not have a felony record, and possess a birth certificate. Applicants who are seventeen years old must have the consent of a parent or legal guardian before entering the service. Enlisted personnel in the Coast Guard must enter active duty before age twenty-eight, whereas enlisted personnel in the Marine Corps must not be over the age of twenty-nine. Applicants must pass a written examination called the Armed Services Vocational Aptitude Battery and meet certain minimum physical standards, such as height, weight, vision, and overall health. All branches of the armed forces require high school graduation or its equivalent for certain enlistment options.

It is a good idea to learn as much as possible about military life before enlisting in the armed forces. Doing so is especially important if you are thinking about making the military a career. Speaking to friends and relatives with military experience can be very helpful. Find out what the military can offer you and what it will expect in return. Then, talk to a recruiter, who can determine whether you qualify for enlistment, explain the various enlistment options, and tell you which military occupational specialties currently have openings. Bear in mind that the recruiter's job is to recruit promising applicants into his or her branch of military service, so the information that the recruiter gives you is likely to stress the positive aspects of military life in the branch in which he or she serves.

Ask the recruiter for the branch you have chosen to assess your chances of being accepted for training in the occupation of your choice, or, better still, take the aptitude exam to see how well you score. The military uses this exam as a placement exam, and test scores largely determine an individual's chances of being accepted into a particular training program. Selection for a particular type of training depends on the needs of the service, your general and technical aptitudes, and your personal preference.

Because all prospective recruits are required to take the exam, those who do so before committing themselves to enlist have the advantage of knowing in advance whether they stand a good chance of being accepted for training in a particular specialty. The recruiter can schedule you for the Armed Services Vocational

Aptitude Battery without any obligation. Many high schools offer the exam as an easy way for students to explore the possibility of a military career, and the test also affords an insight into career areas in which the student has demonstrated aptitudes and interests.

If you decide to join the military, the next step is to pass the physical examination and sign an enlistment contract. Negotiating the contract involves choosing, qualifying for, and agreeing on a number of enlistment options, such as the length of active-duty time, which may vary according to the option. Most active-duty programs have first-term enlistments of four years, although there are some two-, three-, and six-year programs. The contract also will state the date of enlistment and other options—for example, bonuses and the types of training to be received. If the service is unable to fulfill any of its obligations under the contract, such as providing a certain kind of training, the contract may become null and void.

All branches of the armed services offer a delayed-entry program in which an individual can delay entry into active duty for up to one year after enlisting. A high school student can enlist during senior year and enter the service after graduation. Others choose this program because the job training they desire is not currently available but will be within the coming year, or because they need time to arrange their personal affairs.

Women are eligible to enter most military specialties; for example, they may become mechanics, missile maintenance technicians, heavy-equipment operators, and fighter pilots, or they may enter into medical care, administrative support, and intelligence specialties. Generally, only occupations involving direct exposure to combat are excluded.

Those planning to apply the skills gained through military training to a civilian career should first determine how good the prospects are for civilian employment in jobs related to the military specialty that interests them. Second, they should know the prerequisites for the related civilian job. Because many civilian occupations require a license, certification, or minimum level of education, it is important to determine whether military training is sufficient for a person to enter the civilian equivalent or, if not, what additional training will be required. Additional information often can be obtained from school counselors.

Following their enlistment, new members of the armed forces undergo recruit training, better known as basic training. Through courses in military skills and protocol, recruit training provides a six- to twelve-week introduction to military life. Days and nights are carefully structured and include rigorous physical exercise designed to improve strength and endurance and build each unit's cohesion.

Following basic training, most recruits take additional training at technical schools that prepare them for a particular military occupational specialty. The formal training period generally lasts from ten to twenty weeks, although training for certain occupations—nuclear power plant operator, for example—may take as long as a year. Recruits not assigned to classroom instruction receive on-the-job training at their first duty assignment.

Many service people get college credit for the technical training they receive on duty, which, combined with off-duty courses, can lead to an associate's degree through programs in community colleges, such as the Community College of the Air Force.

In addition to on-duty training, military personnel may choose from a variety of educational programs. Most military installations have tuition-assistance programs for people wishing to take courses during off-duty hours. These courses may be correspondence courses or courses in degree programs offered by local colleges or universities. Tuition assistance pays up to 75 percent of college costs. Courses designed to help service personnel earn high school equivalency diplomas are also available.

Each branch of the service provides opportunities for full-time study to a limited number of exceptional applicants. Military personnel accepted into these highly competitive programs—in law or medicine, for example—receive full pay, allowances, tuition, and related fees. In return, they must agree to serve an additional amount of time in the service. Other highly selective programs enable enlisted personnel to qualify as commissioned officers through additional military training.

Officers. Officer training in the armed forces is provided through the several service academies (military, naval, air force, and coast guard); the Reserve Officers Training Corps (ROTC) program offered at many colleges and universities; Officer Candidate School (OCS) or Officer Training School (OTS); the National Guard (State Officer Candidate School programs); the Uniformed Services University of Health Sciences; and other programs. All are highly selective and are good options for those wishing to make the military a career. Candidates interested in obtaining training through the federal service academies must be single to enter and graduate, while those seeking training through OCS, OTS, or ROTC need not be single. Single parents with one or more minor dependents are not eligible to become commissioned officers.

Federal service academies provide a four-year college program leading to a bachelor of science degree. Midshipmen or cadets are provided free room and board, tuition, medical and dental care, and a monthly allowance. Graduates receive regular or reserve commissions and have a five-year active-duty obligation, or more if they are entering flight training.

To become a candidate for appointment as a cadet or midshipman in one of the service academies, applicants are required to obtain a nomination from an authorized source, usually a member of Congress. Candidates do not need to know a member of Congress personally to request a nomination. Nominees must meet academic requirements, have college aptitude test scores above an established minimum, and provide recommendations from teachers or school officials. They also must pass a medical examination. Appointments are made from the list of eligible nominees. Appointments to the Coast Guard Academy, however, are based strictly on merit and do not require a nomination.

ROTC programs train students in about 950 army units, approximately 70 navy and marine units, and around 1,000 air force units at participating colleges and universities. Trainees take two to five hours of military instruction a week in addition to regular college courses. After graduation, they may serve as officers on active duty for a stipulated period. Some may serve their obligation in the reserves or National Guard. In the last two years of an ROTC program, students receive a monthly allowance while attending school, as well as additional pay for summer training. ROTC scholarships for two, three, and four years are available on a competitive basis. All scholarships pay for tuition and have allowances for subsistence, textbooks, supplies, and other costs.

College graduates can earn a commission in the armed forces through OCS or OTS programs in the U.S. Army, Navy, Air Force, Marine Corps, Coast Guard, and National Guard. These officers generally must serve their obligation on active duty. Those with training in certain health professions may qualify for direct appointment as officers. In the case of those studying for the health professions, financial assistance and internship opportunities are available from the military in return for specified periods of military service.

Prospective medical students can apply to the Uniformed Services University of Health Sciences, which offers free tuition in a program leading to an M.D. degree. In return, graduates must serve for seven years in either the military or the U.S. Public Health Service.

Direct appointments also are available for those qualified to serve in other specialty areas, such as the judge advocate general (legal) or chaplain corps. Flight training is available to commissioned officers in each branch of the armed forces. In addition, the army has a direct enlistment option to become a warrant officer aviator.

Each service has different criteria for promoting personnel. Generally, the first few promotions for both enlisted and officer personnel come easily; subsequent promotions are much more competitive. Criteria for promotion may include time in service and in grade, job performance, a fitness report (supervisor's recommendation), and the passing of written examinations. People who are passed over for promotion several times generally must leave the military.

Job Settings

Military personnel are stationed throughout the United States and in many countries around the world. More than half of all military jobs are located in California, Texas, North Carolina, Virginia, Florida, and Georgia. About 395,000 individuals were stationed outside the United States in 2002, including those assigned to ships at sea. Approximately 104,000 of these were stationed in Europe, mainly in Germany, and another 85,000 were assigned to East Asia and the Pacific area, mostly in Japan and the Republic of Korea. Some 211,000 military personnel were deployed to the Middle East in 2003.

Career Outlook

Opportunities should be good for qualified individuals in all branches of the armed forces through 2012. Many military personnel retire with a pension after twenty years of service, while they still are young enough to start a new career. More than 365,000 enlisted personnel and officers must be recruited each year to replace those who complete their commitment or retire. Since the end of the draft in 1973, the military has met its personnel requirements with volunteers. When the economy is good and civilian employment opportunities generally are more favorable, it is more difficult for all the services to meet their recruitment quotas. By contrast, it is much easier to do so during a recession.

America's strategic position is stronger than it has been in decades. Despite reductions in personnel due to the elimination of the threat from Eastern Europe and Russia, the number of active-duty personnel is expected to remain roughly constant through 2012. However, recent conflicts in other countries and the resulting strain on the armed forces may lead to an increasing number of active-duty personnel.

The armed forces' current goal is to maintain a sufficient force to fight and win two major regional conflicts at the same time. Political events, however, could cause these plans to change.

Educational requirements will continue to rise as military jobs become more technical and complex. High school graduates and applicants with college backgrounds will be sought to fill the ranks of enlisted personnel, while virtually all officers will need at least a bachelor's degree and, in some cases, an advanced degree as well.

Earnings for Military Personnel

The earnings structure for military personnel is shown in the following table. Most enlisted personnel started as recruits at Grade E-1 in 2003; however, those with special skills or above-average education started as high as Grade E-4.

Most warrant officers started at Grade W-1 or W-2, depending on their occupational and academic qualifications and branch of service. Because warrant officer is not an entry-level occupation, however, these individuals all had previous military service. Most commissioned officers started at Grade O-1. Some with advanced education started at Grade O-2, and some highly trained officers—for example, physicians and dentists—started as high as Grade O-3.

TABLE 1. Military basic monthly pay by grade for active-duty personnel, June 1, 2003

GRADE	YEARS OF SERVICE					
	Less than 2	More than 4	More than 8	More than 12	More than 16	More than 20
O-10	—	—	—	—	—	$11,875
O-9	—	—	—	—	—	$10,564
O-8	$7,475	$7,927	$8,469	$8,869	$9,238	$10,009
O-7	$6,211	$6,739	$7,121	$7,559	$8,469	$9,051
O-6	$4,603	$5389	$5,641	$5,672	$6,564	$7,233
O-5	$3,838	$4,679	$4,977	$5,403	$5,992	$6,329
O-4	$3,311	$4,146	$4,638	$5,201	$5,471	—
O-3	$2,911	$3,884	$4,274	$4,623	—	—
O-2	$2,515	$3,410	—	—	—	—
O-1	$2,184	$2,747	—	—	—	—
W-5	$5,169	—	—	—	—	—
W-4	$3,088	$3,421	$3,734	$4,045	$4,356	$4,664
W-3	$2,747	$3,018	$3,282	$3,581	$3,916	$4,202
W-2	$2,417	$2,763	$2,993	$3,264	$3,454	$3,706
W-1	$2,134	$2,501	$2,782	$3,007	$3,203	$3,410
E-9	$3,645	$3,687	$4,181	—	—	—
E-8	$2,975	$3,141	$3,342	$3,626	—	—
E-7	$2,069	$2,428	$2,668	$2,838	$3,066	$3,183
E-6	$1,771	$2,117	$2,401	$2,562	$2,663	$2,710
E-5	$1,625	$1,904	$2,152	$2,283	$2,283	—
E-4	$1,503	$1,749	$1,824	—	—	—
E-3	$1,357	$1,529	—	—	—	—
E-2	$1,290	—	—	—	—	—
E-1 4 mo.+	$1,151	—	—	—	—	—
E-1 <4 mo.	$1,065	—	—	—	—	—

Source: U.S. Department of Defense, Defense Finance and Accounting Service (figures rounded to nearest dollar)

Pay varies by total years of service as well as by rank. Because it usually takes many years to reach the higher ranks, most personnel in higher ranks receive the higher pay rates awarded to those with many years of service.

Allowances

In addition to receiving their basic pay, military personnel are provided with free room and board (or a tax-free housing and subsistence allowance), free medical and dental care, a military clothing allowance, military supermarket and department store shopping privileges, thirty days of paid vacation a year (referred to as leave), and travel opportunities.

In many duty stations, military personnel may receive a housing allowance that can be used for off-base housing. This allowance can be substantial but varies greatly by rank and duty station. For example, in July 2003, the housing allowance for an E-4 with dependents was $505 per month; for a comparable individual without dependents, it was $353. The allowance for an O-4 with dependents was $961 per month; for an O-4 person without dependents, it was $836.

Other allowances are paid for foreign duty, hazardous duty, submarine and flight duty, and employment as a medical officer. Athletic and other facilities, such as gymnasiums, tennis courts, golf courses, bowling centers, libraries, and movie theaters, are available on many military installations. Military personnel are eligible for retirement benefits after twenty years of service.

Veterans' Benefits

The Veterans Administration (VA) provides numerous benefits to those who have served at least two years in the armed forces. Veterans are eligible for free care in VA hospitals for service-related disabilities, regardless of time served; those with other medical problems are eligible for free VA care if they are unable to pay the cost of hospitalization elsewhere. Admission to a VA medical center depends on the availability of beds, however.

Veterans also are eligible for certain loans, including loans to purchase a home. Regardless of health, veterans can convert a military life insurance policy to an individual policy with any participating company in the veteran's state of residence. In addition, job counseling, testing, and placement services are available.

Veterans who participate in the New Montgomery GI Bill Program receive educational benefits. Under this program, armed forces personnel may elect to deduct up to $100 a month from their pay during the first twelve months of active duty, putting the money toward their future education. Veterans who serve on active duty for more than two years or who put in two years' active duty plus four years in the Selected Reserve will receive $528 a month in basic benefits for thirty-six months. Those who enlist and serve for two years will receive $429 a month for thirty-six months. In addition, each service provides its own contributions to the enlistee's future education. The sum of the amounts from all of these sources becomes the service member's educational fund. Upon separation from active duty, the fund can be used to finance educational costs at any VA-approved institution. Among those institutions approved by the VA are many vocational, correspondence, certification, business, technical, and flight-training schools; community and junior colleges; and four-year colleges and universities.

A Close-Up Look at Military Careers

Following are the personal observations of three veterans of U.S. military service. Read their accounts to see whether a career in the military is right for you.

Lise Hull, Oceansystems Watch Officer

Lise Hull spent ten years in the United States Navy. She earned a bachelor of arts degree in anthropology from Franklin and

Marshall College in Lancaster, Pennsylvania, and a master's degree in management of public affairs (specializing in historic preservation) from Indiana University in Bloomington. She also holds a master of arts degree (with distinction) in counseling psychology from National University, Sacramento, California, and a master of arts (with distinction) in heritage studies from the University of Wales, Aberystwyth.

The opportunity to enjoy a career and to see the world initially attracted Lise Hull to the U.S. Navy. A counselor at Officer Candidate School gave her a firsthand account of working as an Oceansystems Watch Officer. Hull says, "She talked about how fascinating the work could be in that field and that there were plenty of opportunities to travel. That seemed to be an ideal choice for me!"

Hull joined the navy in 1983 and became commissioned in February 1984. She attended Officer Candidate School in Newport, Rhode Island, as well as additional training courses, including Oceansystems Watch Officer training, CMS Custodian training, and several classes for alcohol and drug counselors.

As an Oceansystems Watch Officer (OWO), Hull worked rotating shifts. She describes the routine: "A 2-2-2-80 rotation is very grueling—two eight-hour shifts from about 7 A.M. to 3 P.M., followed by two eight-hour shifts from 11 P.M. to 7 A.M., and then two eight-hour shifts from 3 P.M. to 11 P.M. After the second day watch, unless something exciting was happening, the shifts blurred together, and on the birdwatchers, it was really tough trying to stay alert. Some watches were busy, others less so. So, we would do drills to keep the sailors prepared for any emergency. Those drills were fun. Some watches were more casual, and the division could relax and talk with each other while still monitoring their work. Others were very intensive, with no time for joking."

Hull particularly enjoyed the ability to form friendships in the navy, describing the different areas where she worked as "like a large family." And although the work was sometimes tedious, she still found it fascinating.

"For me, the ability to be in new places and to travel around the countryside on my days off was the obvious highlight," Hull says. "I got to see Alaska, Great Britain, and California—all places I had never been to before. Also, the pay is great for officers, especially single officers. I could save lots of money, go anywhere, buy pretty much what I want without worrying, but that's not the case for enlisted people."

Hull acknowledges that not everything about military life is positive. As she says, "Of course, there are downsides, too—long days, difficult conditions, restrictions, and expectations. And, as an officer, you have to give the appearance of always being in control and not having any personal problems."

Since retiring from the navy in 1994, Lise Hull has embarked on a career as a freelance writer, castle specialist, and historian with a focus on British heritage and its historical landscape. She credits her navy assignment in Pembrokeshire, Wales, with awakening her interest in the United Kingdom. She established Castles Unlimited, an organization designed to increase awareness of the status of medieval castles in Britain, and is the author of *Countries of the World: Scotland* (Times Media, 2000) and *Castles of Glamorgan* (pending publication).

Christian R. Shaw, Police Officer and U.S. Navy Veteran

Christian R. Shaw attended the Naval Training Center in San Diego, California, in 1985; the Federal Law Enforcement Training Center (FLETC) in Glynco, Georgia, in 1990; the U.S. Navy Fleet Training Center, Small Arms Institute, in San Diego, California, in 1993; and the Veterans Administration Law Enforcement Training Center in Little Rock, Arkansas, in 1993. He then earned an associate's degree in administering to justice and subsequently attended the Los Angeles Police Academy in 1996.

"It all started in 1981, when I joined my high school Junior ROTC," Shaw says. "Then in 1985, I joined the navy with an eight-year-reserve enlistment." His helicopter experiences during that time include helicopter plane captain, aviation shipboard fire-fighter, helicopter utility crewman, and helicopter crew chief.

Shaw also served in the U.S. Army National Guard in California, operated a small private security patrol company, and worked for the Department of Justice as a correctional officer.

He is currently a police officer on patrol in Los Angeles. On his days off, Shaw flies for the California Army National Guard as a helicopter crew chief (also called a flight engineer) in a Blackhawk helicopter. This is a busy schedule, but, as he says, "Flying is hard work, but I love it. It's relaxing to me."

David Winstead, U.S. Air Force Veteran

David Winstead completed his basic military training at Lackland Air Force Base in Texas. He received his technical training at Keesler Air Force Base in Mississippi and secured his security police (law enforcement) training at Davis Monthan Air Force Base in Arizona. He also attended the Command Noncommissioned Officer Academy at Kadena Air Force Base in Japan and took an Advanced Nuclear Weapons Orientation Course at Kirtland Air Force Base in New Mexico.

Winstead explains his decision to join the air force: "I went into the air force right out of high school in 1969. It was during the Vietnam conflict, and it was either join or get drafted. If you joined, you could choose your career and assignment. If you were drafted, you didn't have that choice. Still, the only real reason that I joined was that I felt it was my patriotic duty."

There were many positive aspects of military service for David Winstead. "I found the pluses to be a steady income, rapid advancement, the opportunity to see all of Asia, the chance to make a lot of new friends, and the fact that I had thirty days of leave a year."

Not everything was positive, of course. As he says, "the minuses were the long hours, the necessity for strict adherence to following orders, and the fact that it was difficult on my family."

Advice from the Professionals

Each of these veterans has some advice to offer anyone considering entering military service.

Lise Hull says, "It's important to know that you lose a lot of freedom in the military. You cannot be an individualist and survive. But if you want a career that takes you places and gives you lots of responsibility, this is a great opportunity.

"However, be sure you can conform, that you don't mind working long hours, and that you can keep your opinions to yourself. For me, it's a great way to experience the world and other cultures and personalities. I would advise others to make the most of such opportunities. Explore those locations while you have the chance. You can experience places that most people will never have the chance to."

Christian Shaw offers this observation: "The best part of being in the army is the people you work with and the fun war stories you share. However, there are long hours, and you often have to put up with difficult living conditions."

David Winstead offers this advice: "In one sense, it was a great time, but it was also filled with destruction and horror. I would tell others who are considering military service to be sure that this is what you want. Remember that you need to be willing to give your life for your country because you never know when you might be asked to do just that."

For Additional Information

The following websites provide extensive information about branches of the military.

United States Department of Defense
www.defenselink.mil

United States Army
www.goarmy.com

U.S. Military Academy, West Point
www.usma.edu

Army ROTC
goarmy.com/rotc

Army Reserve
www.armyreserve.army.mil

Army National Guard
www.arng.army.mil

United States Air Force
www.af.mil

U.S. Air Force Academy, Colorado Springs
www.usafa.af.mil

Air Force ROTC
www.afrotc.com

Air Force Reserve
www.afreserve.com

Air National Guard
www.goang.com

United States Coast Guard
www.uscg.mil

U.S. Coast Guard Academy, New London
www.cga.edu

Coast Guard Reserve
www.uscg.mil/reserve

United States Marine Corps
www.usmc.mil

Marine Corps Reserve
www.marforres.usmc.mil

United States Navy
www.navy.com

U.S. Naval Academy, Annapolis
www.nadn.navy.mil

Navy ROTC
www.nrotc.navy.mil

Navy Reserve
www.navalreserve.com

CHAPTER FIVE

Careers in Politics and Government

Politics is the art of the possible.
—Otto von Bismarck

If a job in government or politics is of interest to you, this chapter will show you that you can pursue such a career at the local, state, and federal levels.

Government jobs are available in the following areas: agriculture, animal control, aquariums and zoos, code administration and enforcement, computers, engineering and science, environment, fire protection, fleet and facilities management, forestry and horticulture, law enforcement, legal services and the courts, library services, media and the arts, parks and recreation, planning, community and economic development, housing, landscape architecture, public administration, public health and health care, public safety, public works, records management, social services, transportation and traffic, and utilities management.

Elected Officials

At the top of the political hierarchy are public officeholders, including mayors, governors, supervisors, senators, representatives, and, of course, the president and vice president of the country. All of these individuals are elected to administer government.

They handle the business of a city, town, county, state, or the country as a whole. They must pass laws to keep order, set up special programs to benefit people, and spend the taxpayers' money on goods and services. As problem solvers, they meet with community leaders to determine the needs of the people, and then they search for ways to meet those needs.

There are many other levels of political careers—all the way down to grassroots levels. This would include those who work for political change in their neighborhoods and those who serve in an official capacity, such as precinct captain. Several of these jobs are voluntary, unpaid positions that could eventually lead to paying positions.

All political positions except appointed government managers are elected by their constituents. Nonelected managers are hired by a local government council or commission.

Chief Executives and Legislators

Government chief executives, like their counterparts in the private sector, have overall responsibility for the operation of their organizations. Working with legislators, they set goals and arrange programs to attain them. They appoint department heads to oversee the civil servants who carry out programs enacted by legislative bodies. Chief executives in government oversee budgets and ensure that resources are used properly and that programs are carried out as planned.

The duties of government chief executives also include meeting with legislators and constituents to determine the level of support for proposed programs. In addition, they often nominate citizens to boards and commissions, encourage business investment, and promote economic development in their communities. To do all of these varied tasks effectively, chief executives of large governments rely on a staff of highly skilled aides to research issues that concern the public. Executives who control small governmental bodies, however, often do this work by themselves.

Legislators are elected officials who develop, enact, or amend laws. They include United States senators and representatives, state senators and representatives, and county, city, and town commissioners and council members.

Legislators introduce, examine, and vote on bills to pass official legislation. In preparing such legislation, they study staff reports and hear testimony from constituents, representatives of interest groups, board and commission members, and others with an interest in the issue under consideration. They usually must approve budgets and the appointments of nominees for leadership posts whose names are submitted by the chief executive. In some bodies, the legislative council appoints the city, town, or county manager.

Both chief executives and legislators perform many ceremonial duties, such as opening new buildings, making proclamations, welcoming visitors, and leading celebrations. It is both a privilege and an important responsibility to serve in public office.

State and Local Government

State and local governments provide their constituents with vital services, such as transportation, public safety, health care, education, utilities, and courts. Excluding education and hospitals, state and local governments employ about 7.9 million workers, placing them among the largest employers in the economy. Around two-thirds of these employees work for local governments, such as counties, cities, special districts, and towns.

In addition to fifty state governments, there are about 87,500 local governments, according to the U.S. Census Bureau. These include about 3,000 county governments, 19,400 municipal governments, 16,500 townships, 13,500 school districts, and 35,100 special districts. Illinois has the most local government units, with more than 6,900; Hawaii has the fewest, with 20.

In many areas of the country, citizens are served by more than one local government unit. For example, most states have counties, which usually contain various cities or towns and often include unincorporated rural areas. Townships, which often contain suburban or rural areas, may include municipalities. Supplementing these forms of local government, special district government bodies are independent, limited-purpose governmental units that usually perform a single function or activity. For example, a large percentage of special districts manage the use of natural resources. Some provide drainage and flood control, irrigation, and soil and water conservation services.

Jobs in State and Local Government

The majority of jobs in state and local government are in service occupations, which account for 31 percent of all jobs in this category. The largest occupations are police and sheriff's patrol officers, bailiffs, correctional officers and jailers, and firefighters.

Professional and related occupations account for 21 percent of employment in state and local government; office and administrative support occupations account for 20 percent; and management, business, and financial occupations constitute 11 percent.

State and local governments employ people in occupations found in nearly every industry in the economy, including chief executives, managers, engineers, computer specialists, secretaries, and health technicians. Certain occupations, however, are mainly or exclusively found in these governments, such as legislators; tax examiners, collectors, and revenue agents; urban and regional planners; and judges, magistrates, and other judicial workers.

At the state and local levels, chief executives include governors, lieutenant governors, mayors, and city managers. General and operations managers include district managers and revenue directors. Legislators include state senators and representatives, county commissioners, and city council members.

Tax examiners, collectors, and revenue agents determine tax liability and collect past-due taxes from individuals or businesses.

Urban and regional planners draft plans and recommend programs for the development and use of resources, such as land and water. They also propose construction of physical facilities, such as schools and roads, under the authority of their municipality. Planners devise strategies outlining the best use of community land and identify the places in which residential, commercial, recreational, and other types of development should be located.

Judges arbitrate, advise, and administer justice in a court of law. They oversee legal processes in courts and apply the law to resolve civil disputes and determine guilt in criminal cases. Magistrates resolve criminal cases not involving penitentiary sentences, as well as civil cases involving damages below a sum specified by state law.

Court, municipal, and license clerks perform a variety of state and local government administrative tasks. Court clerks prepare dockets of cases to be called; secure information for judges; and contact witnesses, lawyers, and attorneys to obtain information for the court. Municipal clerks draft agendas for town or city councils, record minutes of council meetings, answer official correspondence, keep fiscal records and accounts, and prepare reports on civic needs. License clerks keep records and help the public obtain motor vehicle ownership titles, operator permits, and a variety of other permits and licenses. State and local governments also employ many secretaries, administrative assistants, and general office workers.

Highway workers are state or local government employees who maintain highways, municipal and rural roads, airport runways, and rights-of-way. They patch broken or eroded pavement, repair guardrails and highway markers, plow snow, and mow or clear brush from along roads.

Bus drivers may be employed by local governments or private companies. They pick up and deliver passengers at prearranged stops throughout their assigned routes. Drivers may collect fares, answer questions about bus schedules and transfer points, and announce stops.

The duties of law enforcement officers and firefighters, who are often employed by state and local governments, are discussed in Chapters 2 and 3, respectively.

Training for State and Local Government Jobs

The education level and experience needed by workers in state and local governments varies by occupation. Voters elect most chief executives and legislators, so local support is very important. Taking part in volunteer work and helping to provide community services are valuable ways to establish vital community support.

Those elected to chief executive and legislator positions come from a variety of backgrounds but must conform to age, residency, and citizenship regulations regarding the positions that they seek. Advancement opportunities for most elected public officials are limited to other offices in the jurisdictions in which they live. For example, a local council member may run for mayor or for a position in state government, and a state legislator may decide to run for governor or for the United States Congress.

A master's degree in public administration is widely recommended, but not required, for a position as city manager. Candidates may gain experience as management analysts or assistants in government departments, working with councils and mayors. After several years, they may be hired to manage a town or a small city and eventually become managers of larger cities.

A college degree is required for most professional jobs. For entry-level urban or regional planning positions, most state and local government agencies require two years of graduate study in urban and regional planning or the equivalent in work experience.

To become a judge, particularly a state trial or appellate court judge, one usually is required to be a lawyer. About half of all state judges are appointed, and the other half are elected in partisan or nonpartisan elections. Most state and local judges serve fixed terms, ranging from four or six years for limited-jurisdiction judges to fourteen years for some appellate court judges.

Bus drivers must comply with federal regulations that require drivers who operate vehicles designed to transport sixteen or more passengers to obtain a commercial driver's license from the state in which they live. To qualify for a commercial driver's license, applicants must pass a written test on rules and regulations and demonstrate that they can operate a commercial vehicle safely.

For subway and streetcar operator jobs, applicants with at least a high school education have the best chance. In some cities, prospective subway operators are required to work as bus drivers for a specified period. Successful applicants generally are in good health, possess good communication skills, and are able to make quick, sound judgments. Because bus drivers and subway operators deal with passengers, they need an even temperament and emotional stability. Driving in heavy, fast-moving, or stop-and-go traffic and dealing with passengers can be stressful.

The job requirements for police officers and firefighters are covered in detail in Chapters 2 and 3.

Federal Government Jobs

The federal government employs workers in almost every occupation, with about three out of four working in professional; management, business, and financial; or office and administrative support occupations. A highly systematized hiring program offers positions in the following five general categories:

- Professional occupations
- Administrative occupations
- Technical occupations
- Clerical occupations
- Other occupations

SAMPLE FEDERAL JOB ANNOUNCEMENT

Vacancy Announcement: Department of the Navy, Navy Field Offices

Position: Accountant, Accountant/Supervisory

Series and Grade: GS-0510 to 0512

Salary: $28,090–$94,306 annually

Duty Location: Many vacancies in the Philadelphia Metro Area, Pennsylvania

Who May Apply: Status/Federal Civil Service Employees

How to Apply. Visit the website at www.donhr.navy.mil/jobs/categorydefinitions.asp for a list of definitions on the following hiring categories: current federal employees serving under a career or career-conditional appointment in the competitive service; former federal employees with reinstatement eligibility; Interagency Career Transition Assistance Plan (ICTAP) eligibles; persons eligible for noncompetitive appointment under special authorities; or preference eligibles or veterans who have been honorably separated from the armed forces after substantially completing an initial three-year term of active service. Selecting official may choose to limit consideration to subgroups of those who apply. Candidates whose current or previous permanent position is at the same grade level, or at a higher grade level, than the announced position (or its target) and who meet the qualification requirements will be referred to the Selecting Official as noncompetitive candidates.

Major Duties. The duties of the position involve advising on, administering, and/or performing professional accounting work relating to the financial activities of the government. The work includes the design, development, operation, or inspection of accounting systems; the prescription of accounting standards, policies, and requirements; the examination, analysis, and interpretation of accounting data, records, or reports; or the provision of accounting or financial management advice and assistance to management.

As a supervisor, is responsible for carrying out EEO policies to assure that qualifications, determinations, selections, work assignments, training, promotions, details, discipline, and awards are made/given without regard to race, color, religion, sex, age, national origin, handicap, or disabled veteran status. Cooperates and participates fully in the development of affirmative action program plans. Deals effectively with employees and union representatives on employee suggestions, complaints, grievances, and other matters involved in the day-to-day administration of labor-management agreements, sometimes including labor-management contract negotiations. Reviews the work of subordinates and assesses progress against goals and makes adjustments as necessary; coordinates/negotiates changes to policy and/or program requirements with senior personnel locally and with other activities, commands, and agencies.

Qualifications Required. All eligibility and qualification requirements must be met by the referral date. Applicants must meet time in grade requirements as described by 5 CFR 300 Subpart F. Positions may include individual occupational requirements or positive educational requirements. Please refer to OPM Qualification Standards Operating Manual for general schedule positions Part III Index at www.opm.gov/qualifications/index.htm.

Some positions may be covered under the Defense Acquisition Workforce Improvement Act (DAWIA) and require additional education, training, and experience. Applicants not certified may apply but must achieve certification within eighteen months of appointment. Certification requirements may be viewed at www.dau.mil/career/appc.htm.

How You Will Be Evaluated. Resumes are evaluated by an automated system (RESUMIX) that matches the skills extracted from the candidate's resume to the skills identified for the position. In addition, other requirements (time-in-grade, education, area of consideration, specialized experience) must be met to determine the qualified candidates referred to the selecting official for consideration.

How to Apply. Please visit our webpage at www.donhr.navy.mil/HRSC/northeast/localnews.htm for additional information and helpful tips on applying for positions serviced by our region. An automated inventory referral system (RESUMIX) is used to fill vacancies through the Merit Promotion Program and other noncompetitive means. When applying, carefully follow the instructions below to ensure you receive consideration for the position.

A resume and an Additional Data Sheet (ADS) are required for this position. If you have a current up-to-date resume and ADS on file with the Human Resources Service Center, Northeast, you may use Application Express on the DONHR website at www.donhr.navy.mil/jobs.

Otherwise, you may apply through the Department of the Navy Online Resume Builder (preferred method) at www.donhr.navy.mil/jobs.

The resume builder will properly format and submit your resume; resumes are normally processed within three days.

If for some reason you are unable to access our DON Resume Builder, you can submit your resume and Additional Data Sheet responses via mail. Hardcopy resumes are normally processed within two weeks of receipt. Mail your completed resume, ADS, and any requested additional documents to: Human Resources Service Center, Northeast, ATTN: RESUMIX, 111 South Independence Mall East, Philadelphia, PA. 19106.

More Government Job Opportunities

Jobs with the federal government also include working for the various departments of government, such as the Department of Agriculture, the Department of Defense, the Department of Justice, the Department of Homeland Security, the Department of State, the United States Treasury Department, the Department of Veterans Affairs, and many others.

Each major department includes a number of subdepartments. The Department of the Interior, for instance, includes the Fish and Wildlife Service, the Bureau of Indian Affairs, the Bureau of Land Management, and the National Park Service. Opportunities for government or political jobs may be found throughout the country in federal, state, and local offices.

Working Conditions

The working conditions of legislators and government chief executives vary with the size and budget of the governmental unit. Time spent at work ranges from a few hours a week for some local leaders to stressful weeks of sixty or more hours for members of the U.S. Congress. Similarly, some jobs require only occasional out-of-town travel, while others involve long periods away from home, such as when attending sessions of the legislature.

United States senators and representatives, governors and lieutenant governors, and chief executives and legislators in municipalities work full-time, year-round, as do most county and city managers. Many state legislators work full-time on government business while the legislature is in session (usually for two to six months a year or every other year) and work only part-time when the legislature is not in session.

Some local elected officials work a schedule that is officially designated as part-time but actually is the equivalent of a full-time schedule when unpaid duties are taken into account. In addition to their regular schedules, most chief executives are on call to handle emergencies.

Given the wide range of federal jobs, most of the working conditions found in the private sector also are found in the federal government. Most white-collar employees work in office buildings, hospitals, or laboratories, and most of the blue-collar workforce can be found in warehouses, shipyards, military bases, construction sites, national parks, and national forests. Work environments vary from comfortable and relaxed to hazardous and stressful, such as those experienced by law enforcement officers, astronauts, and air traffic controllers.

The vast majority of federal employees work full-time, often on flexible or "flexi-time" schedules that allow workers more control over their work schedules. Some agencies also offer telecommuting or "flexi-place" programs, which allow selected workers to perform some job duties at home or from regional centers.

Some federal workers spend much of their time away from their offices. Inspectors and compliance officers, for example, often visit businesses and work sites to ensure that laws and regulations are obeyed. Some federal workers frequently travel long distances, spending days or weeks away from home. Auditors, for example, may spend weeks at a time in distant locations.

Qualifications and Training

Apart from meeting minimum age, residency, and citizenship requirements, candidates for legislative positions have no established training or qualifications criteria. Candidates come from a wide variety of occupations, such as lawyer, private sector manager or executive, or business owner. Many have some political experience as staffers or members of government bureaus, boards, or commissions. Successful candidates usually become well known through their political campaigns, and some have built voter name recognition through their work with community, religious, fraternal, or social organizations.

Increasingly, candidates target information to voters through advertising paid for by their respective campaigns, so fund-raising skills are essential to those hoping to win an election. Volunteering in public service and gaining work experience at the management level help to develop the fund-raising, budgeting, public speaking, and problem-solving skills that are needed to run an effective political campaign.

Candidates must be able to make decisions quickly, sometimes on the basis of limited or contradictory information. They also should be able to inspire and motivate their constituents and staff. Additionally, they must know how to reach compromises and satisfy the often conflicting demands of their constituents. National, state, and many local campaigns require massive amounts of energy and stamina, traits vital to successful candidates.

Virtually all town, city, and county managers have at least a bachelor's degree, and many hold a higher degree. A master's degree in public administration is recommended, including courses in public financial management and legal issues in public administration.

Working in management-support positions in government is a prime source of the experience and personal contacts required to eventually secure a management position. For example, applicants often gain experience as management analysts or assistants in government departments, working for committees, councils, or chief executives. In this capacity, they learn about planning, budgeting, civil engineering, and other aspects of running a government. With sufficient experience, they may be hired to manage a small government.

Town, city, or county managers generally start by working in a smaller community and advancing to larger municipalities as they gain experience. A broad knowledge of local issues, combined with communication skills and the ability to compromise, are essential for advancement in this field.

Advancement opportunities for elected officials are not clearly defined. Because elected positions normally require a period of residency and because local public support is critical, officials usually advance to other offices through new elections for higher offices, most often in the jurisdictions where they live. For example, council members may run for mayor or for a position in the state government, and state legislators may run for governor or for the U.S. Congress or Senate.

Many officials are not politically ambitious, however, and do not seek advancement. Others lose their bids for reelection or voluntarily leave the occupation. A lifetime career as a government chief executive or legislator is rare.

In the federal government, each department or agency determines its own training requirements and offers workers opportunities to improve job skills or become qualified to advance to other jobs. These opportunities may include technical or skills training; tuition assistance or reimbursement; fellowship programs; and executive leadership and management training programs, seminars, and workshops. This training may be offered on the job, by another agency, or at local colleges and universities.

Advancement in the federal government is commonly based on a system of occupational pay levels, or "grades." Workers enter the federal civil service at the starting grade for an occupation and follow a career ladder of promotions until they reach the full-performance grade for that occupation. This system provides for a limited number of noncompetitive promotions, which usually are awarded at regular intervals, assuming job performance is satisfactory.

Although these promotions do not occur more than once a year, they sometimes are awarded in the form of two-grade increases. For example, in some cases, a worker may advance from grade 7 to 9 in the first year, from grade 9 to 11 in the second year, and from grade 11 to 12 in the third year. The exact pay grades associated with a job's career track depend upon the occupation.

Typically, workers without a high school diploma who are hired as clerks start at grade 1, and high school graduates with no additional training hired at the same job start at grade 2 or 3. Entrants who have some technical training or experience and are hired as technicians may start at grade 4. Those with a bachelor's degree generally are hired in professional occupations, such as economist, with a career ladder that starts at grade 5 or 7, depending on academic achievement. Entrants with a master's degree or doctorate may start at grade 9. Individuals with professional degrees may be hired at the grade 11 or 12 level.

New employees usually start at the first step of a grade; however, if the position in question is difficult to fill, entrants may receive somewhat higher pay or special rates. Almost all physician and engineer positions, for example, fall into this category.

Workers who advance to managerial or supervisory positions may receive within-grade longevity increases, bonuses, and promotions to higher grades. The top managers in the federal civil service belong to the Senior Executive Service (SES), the highest positions that federal workers can reach without being specifically nominated by the president and confirmed by the U.S. Senate. Relatively few workers attain SES positions, and competition is intense.

Bonuses for SES positions are even more performance-based than are those for lower-level positions. Because it is the headquarters for most federal agencies, the Washington, D.C., metropolitan area offers the best opportunities to advance to upper-level managerial and supervisory jobs.

Salaries for Elected Officials

Earnings of public administrators vary widely, depending on the size of the government unit and on whether the job is part-time, full-time and year-round, or full-time for only a few months a year. Salaries range from little or nothing for a council member in a small town to $400,000 a year for the president of the United States.

The National Conference of State Legislatures reports that the annual salary for legislators in the forty states that paid annual salaries ranged from $10,000 to $99,000 or more in 2003. In eight states, legislators received a daily salary plus an additional allowance for living expenses while legislatures were in session.

The Council of State Governments reports in its *Book of the States, 2002–2003* that gubernatorial annual salaries ranged from $50,000 in American Samoa to $179,000 in New York. In addition to a salary, most governors received benefits such as transportation and an official residence.

In 2003, U.S. senators and representatives earned $154,700; the senate and house majority and minority leaders earned $171,900, and the vice president was paid $198,600.

Median annual earnings of legislators were $15,220 in 2002. The middle 50 percent earned between $13,180 and $38,540. The lowest 10 percent earned less than $12,130, and the highest 10 percent earned more than $69,380.

Salaries for Federal Jobs

There are several pay systems governing the salary rates of federal civilian employees. The majority of federal workers are paid under the General Schedule (GS), which has fifteen grades of pay for civilian white-collar and service workers and smaller within-grade step increases that occur based on length of service and quality of performance.

Workers in cities with high costs of living are paid as much as an additional 21 percent, and some hard-to-fill occupations are paid more as an incentive. In general, this schedule is amended every January to reflect changes in the cost of living. Following are the 2004 annual starting salaries for the GS grades:

GS-1	$15,625	GS-9	$36,478
GS-2	$17,568	GS-10	$40,171
GS-3	$19,168	GS-11	$44,136
GS-4	$21,518	GS-12	$52,899
GS-5	$24,075	GS-13	$62,905
GS-6	$26,836	GS-14	$74,335
GS-7	$29,821	GS-15	$87,439
GS-8	$33,026		

The Federal Wage System (FWS) is used to pay most federal workers in craft, repair, operator, and laborer jobs. This schedule sets federal wages so that they are comparable with prevailing regional wage rates for similar types of jobs. As a result, wage rates paid under the FWS can vary significantly from one locality to another.

In addition to base pay and bonuses, federal employees may receive incentive awards. These one-time awards, ranging from $25 to $10,000, are bestowed for a significant suggestion, a special act or service, or sustained high job performance. Some workers also may receive "premium" pay, which is granted when the employee must work overtime, on holidays, on weekends, at night, or under hazardous conditions.

Benefits are an important part of federal employee compensation. Federal employees may choose from a number of health plans and life insurance options, and premium payments for these policies are partially offset by the government.

In addition, workers hired after January 1, 1984, participate in the Federal Employees Retirement System (FERS), a three-tiered retirement plan including Social Security, a pension plan, and an optional Thrift Savings Plan. Employee participation in the Thrift Savings Plan is voluntary, but any contributions made are tax-deferred and, up to a point, matched by the federal government. In addition to other benefits, some federal agencies provide public transit subsidies in an effort to encourage employee use of public transportation.

Federal employees receive both vacation and sick leave. They earn thirteen days of vacation leave a year for the first three years, twenty days a year for the next twelve years, and twenty-six days a year after their fifteenth year of service. Workers also receive thirteen days of sick leave a year, which may be accumulated indefinitely. About a third of all federal civilian employees are union members or covered by union contract, more than double the proportion of workers in all industries.

A Close-Up Look at Jobs in Government and Politics

Following are the personal accounts of a federal employee and three people who work in different aspects of politics. Perhaps their experiences will spark your interest in government.

Karen Sweeny-Justice, National Park Ranger

Karen Sweeny-Justice earned an A.A.S. degree in graphic art from Onondaga Community College in Syracuse, New York; an A.A. in communications from Cazenovia College in Cazenovia, New York; and a B.S. in human development from Syracuse University in New York.

She served as a national park ranger for interpretative programs at Big South Fork National River and Recreation Area, Tennessee, and in Kentucky. Karen was associated with the park service for more than twelve years, during which she completed a number of courses with the National Park Service and National Career Workshops, including Developing African-American Interpretive Programs, Interpretation for Children, Self-Study Course for Interpreters, Interpretation in Urban Areas, Ranger Skills, How to Supervise People, Management Skills for Success in the 1990s,

How to Work with People, and Orientation to the Management of National Park System Resources, as well as first aid and safety courses.

"After working in a bank as a financial sales counselor for more than two years, I decided I needed a change," Sweeny-Justice says, "so I quit that job and, sight unseen, accepted a position for a lot less money as a summer employee at the Old Faithful Lodge in Yellowstone National Park. I used the chance to be in the park as a basis for exploration of the region, and, discovering that I was one of the 'older' concession employees (at the ripe old age of twenty-eight), I decided I needed something that would get me out of the dorm. So when I learned that the park service needed volunteers, I signed on to work at the Old Faithful Visitor Center. The rangers I worked with were informative and trusted me enough to let me solo on explanations of what was going on. I even got good at predicting when Old Faithful would erupt."

Sweeny-Justice decided to volunteer with the Student Conservation Association and was selected by Biscayne National Park to spend the winter in Florida. On this assignment, she did much of the work performed by seasonal park rangers, including presenting programs to the public and staffing the visitor center. She found that she liked helping visitors to better understand and appreciate the parks.

"There was nothing in my past experience that would have indicated that I'd like parks," she says. "I grew up in a city and am the only one of my family that has left. And not only have I left my hometown, I've traveled and worked in a variety of locations in the past twelve years, including Yellowstone, Biscayne, Shenandoah, Lowell, Valley Forge, and Big South Fork."

A park ranger's workday varies depending on which park he or she works in. Sweeny-Justice explains that some parks are busier than others, based on their location and the seasonal attractions. As she says, "Yellowstone is mostly summer, while the Everglades is mostly winter. It all depends on the weather and natural conditions. So, some days it may be boring and slow, allowing lots of time to do research, while on other days one may not even get a chance for lunch.

Her work with interpretative programs isn't dangerous, but, on occasion, she may be asked to help with medical emergencies and search and rescues. "Some parks have different shifts that need to be covered, and sometimes that means opening or closing buildings alone," she explains.

The typical work week is forty hours, but overtime is possible if the park is understaffed. In addition, working with the public can sometimes be stressful. Sweeny-Justice says, "Each park does get its share of visitors who think that because rangers are public servants, they can be walked over, ignored, or abused. It doesn't happen often, but it does happen. I've had people shout and yell at me and call me names. On the other hand, I've received lots of praise from people who have enjoyed the programs I've done well enough to send letters to my supervisors."

Despite the occasional unpleasant visitor, however, Sweeny-Justice finds positive aspects of the job. "The upsides of the job are the feelings that come when you can see someone grasping a concept they didn't understand before or helping someone to make the most of a visit. Getting to see the treasures our nation offers is a benefit, too. It used to be said that rangers were 'paid in sunsets.'

"The downsides are the fact that the pay isn't spectacular, people don't always use their common sense when they're on vacation, and there is a lot of work in buildings that can be very uncomfortable. For example, I worked year-round in historic Washington's Headquarters at Valley Forge. The building was built in the eighteenth century, didn't have a modern heating/cooling system, and had only one bare lightbulb hanging in the stairwell behind the door to the basement. Needless to say, it wasn't very comfortable."

Karen Sweeny-Justice has left the national park service and now works as a freelance writer. Her love of national parks and historic sites has not left her, however. Karen works part-time as an interpretive tour guide at Historic Rugby, Inc., an 1880s British village located in eastern Tennessee. She has also published many feature and travel articles, and her books include *Port Kennedy: A Village in the Shadow of Valley Forge* (Thomas Publications) and *Valley Forge for Kids of All Ages*, an activity book.

Vera Marie Badertscher, Campaign Manager and Campaign Consultant

Vera Marie Badertscher earned both B.A. and B.S. degrees in education from Ohio State University in 1960. She went on to secure an M.F.A. from Arizona State University in 1976, focusing on theater. Early in her career, Badertscher worked primarily as a campaign manager but later switched to campaign consultant. She currently works as a freelance writer.

"I started as a citizen volunteer in city projects," she explains. "As a young mother, I wanted a better library system in Scottsdale, Arizona, where I lived, so I volunteered for a committee. There I met officeholders, was invited to serve on advisory committees, and eventually asked for and received pay for managing a city council election campaign.

"I enjoyed the sense of accomplishment I got from working in politics—of being able to promote my beliefs and make things happen," Badertscher says. "I also enjoyed the fact that most people involved in politics are action oriented, optimistic true believers. My chief asset was an ability to figure out the best way to communicate political messages and move people to action."

Badertscher did volunteer work in a federated woman's club, an experience that taught her a great deal. Here she gained valuable experience, including "bringing diverse people together to work on projects; combining government and private energies;

communicating; and organizing projects. My theater background helped me focus on short-term, collaborative projects."

As a campaign manager, Badertscher spent most of her working time communicating with volunteers, either by telephone or in memos and newsletters. The limited time of a political campaign makes the job very intense, and quick decision making becomes a vital part of a campaign manager's duties. She says, "Someone advised me when I managed my first congressional campaign that during the last couple of weeks of the campaign, I would be making a dozen decisions every hour, and one in twenty or so would be truly important."

In addition, a successful campaign manager must also be able to prioritize. It is important to know the difference between decisions that do not affect the outcome of an election and those that do.

Badertscher summarizes the job: "A campaign manager rounds up diverse interest groups, volunteers, the candidate and his or her family, advertising personnel, researchers, and fund-raisers. The key to being successful is keeping the focus on what will get the candidate elected and not allowing anyone in the campaign to draw the focus in another direction. You can expect to talk on the phone all day, check off on other people's work, and stay close to the candidate to keep him or her on track. Generally, you are trying to keep the budget down, so the work surroundings are on the primitive side—borrowed furniture and unpainted walls. You can count on noise and constant activity. (If it's quiet, you're probably losing.) This presents a hard atmosphere to concentrate in, but that's the job."

The work of a campaign consultant, by contrast, is somewhat less hectic. She says, "A campaign consultant has more luxury of time to think than does a campaign manager. The consultant typically analyzes voting data history; studies the candidate, the opponent, and the voters; and writes a strategic plan for bringing the voters to support that candidate. Some consultants specialize in media or mail, but I have been a generalist, doing strategy and writing direct mail. The consultant works in an office or home office and meets weekly or biweekly with the candidate, the campaign manager, and others involved in the campaign. Once the plan is written, the consultant is available to help with fine-tuning, to help make adjustments, to help review media plans, to help determine what to ask in polling, and to help interpret the results. While the campaign manager's job is not done until the polls close on election day, the consultant's job is done a few days prior to the election when no more mail can be sent or advertising launched that will affect the outcome."

Badertscher is frank about the aspects of her job that she likes and dislikes. "I most like the ability to work out the puzzles involved in bringing together the circumstances, the candidate, and the voters in order to persuade them that they will be better off to elect that candidate. I like the thinking and the communicating of politics.

"What I least like is having to be nice to a bunch of people that I might not particularly like or admire. However, I have been fortunate in being able to choose the candidates I work for, so I have worked for people I believe in and personally support. However, politics is about coalition building, so sometimes the expression 'politics makes strange bedfellows' is all too true."

Wade Hyde, Political Consultant

Wade Hyde earned a B.A. in education and history from East Texas State University in Commerce, Texas. He then received an M.A. in urban affairs from the University of Texas at Arlington and an M.A. in civic affairs teaching from the University of Dallas in Irving, Texas. He has served as a campaign manager and volunteer consultant, as a civic volunteer board member, and as a planning and zoning commission member in Irving, Texas. Hyde has also served as a member of the regional transportation board and member and officer of the Visiting Nurses Association.

"In 1980, I began volunteering in organizations supporting interests with legislative agendas," Hyde says. "Political events were at the center of what I found to be most interesting and exciting in earlier years. These events included listening to the presidential nominating conventions on the radio (before pollsters and analysts took all the fun and suspense out of final outcomes) and waiting in the town square for the results of local elections on hot Saturday nights in June.

"History studies and government were naturally interesting and easy for me. No other subject particularly intrigued me. Politics and policy are my calling."

Hyde explains that there are different types of political campaigns. The work is seasonal, although the type of campaign (local, regional, or national) determines whether the season lasts three months or two years. Local campaigns usually last about three months, so the job is very intense with the work concentrated into a short time. The fact that many candidates in local elections know very little about such issues as fund-raising, coalition building, or voter lists makes the campaign manager's job even more stressful.

"The nature of the political candidate is usually one of tremendous energy and strong ego with an unshakable belief that the voting populace cannot live without his or her leadership," he says. "The consultant, on the other hand, must bring some order and a consistent, coherent message to the candidate and the workers. The atmosphere is one of chaotic, pressure-cooker days and nights."

Given the intensity of the work, it is not surprising that Hyde would acknowledge some negative aspects of the job. As he says, "Everything is always late, unexpected, and includes last-minute and last-second decision making—sometimes like flipping a coin and forging ahead or backtracking. The days start as if the nights had never quit, and each workday lasts about eighteen hours. Both the candidate and campaign workers contract battle fatigue that doesn't end until weeks after election day. Saturdays and Sundays are not exempt."

Fortunately, there is a bright side to the challenges of being a political consultant. "Each new campaign and candidate comes with the promise of a better day and a better way. It's exciting and hopeful to be involved in making a positive change by helping elect someone who can make a big difference. At least that's the upside. The downside is the exhaustion and condensed pressure of a compact campaign effort and, if such should occur, the loss of the candidate's best effort."

K. Mark Takai, State Representative

K. Mark Takai earned a bachelor of arts degree in political science in 1990 and a master of public health degree in health education in 1993 from the University of Hawaii at Manoa. During his internship for his master's degree, he worked for a city council member for the city and county of Honolulu.

"My experiences at the University of Hawaii while an undergraduate student, graduate student, and employee probably attracted me to the state capitol," he says. "It was through these years that I had the most interaction with the legislators. I now serve as an elected state representative for District 34, which includes part of Aiea and part of Pearl City (both located near Pearl Harbor on Oahu)."

Takai became interested in elected office when he was involved in student government in fourth grade. This involvement continued through high school and college, where he served as student body president representing twenty-four hundred students and twelve thousand students, respectively. He declared his candidacy for public office in July 1994, won the primary election in September, and was declared the winner of the seat after the general election in November.

"The job of a state representative runs the gamut," Takai says. "There are probably three different 'jobs' of an elected official—

very diverse, but all very important. The first is my job as a community leader. This is probably the most rewarding part of being in public office. The interaction with the community—through the schools, community organizations, neighborhood board meetings, and so forth—all provide me with the opportunity to listen and then respond to the desires and concerns of the public.

"This part of the job can also be very difficult. I have been very fortunate in that I have not had too many difficult meetings with the public; however, as a freeway project is currently being planned and the project calls for possible public condemnation of private property, I have had my fair share of angry constituents. Most times, though, I am able to work with the residents of our community to address their concerns.

"The second part of my job is as a lawmaker. Constitutionally, this is my most important responsibility. Seventy-five legislators decide what laws are passed.

"My third responsibility is as a politician (i.e., a political candidate). This is a very time-consuming process. The 'campaign season' begins around July of even-numbered years and doesn't end until the general election in early November. Aside from raising money to run a successful campaign (marketing materials, brochures, advertisements, and so on), the most difficult and time-consuming tasks of the political season are sign waving (waving to cars along the roadside in the mornings and afternoons) and door-to-door canvassing." (Since winning his first election in 1994, Mark has run four successful reelection campaigns for a two-year office.)

Takai's typical workday depends on the time of year. During the legislative session, from January to May, he begins his day with a 7:30 A.M. breakfast meeting, followed by committee meetings at the state capitol beginning by 9 A.M. The legislators hold private meetings in their offices and catch up on phone calls and messages prior to the House floor session at noon. He eats lunch with constituents or attends a luncheon meeting after the floor session.

Committee hearings begin at 2 P.M. and last until 7 P.M. The day usually ends with community meetings that run until about 10 P.M. Saturdays are generally spent at committee hearings or community events. Takai reserves Friday evenings and Sundays for time with his family.

The months when the legislature is not in session or he is not running a reelection do not necessarily afford slow workdays. As Takai says, "I usually work in the office planning for upcoming events. As the state cochairman of Hawaii's Children and Youth in October and as the state chairman of Hawaii's Junior Miss Scholarship Program, I find myself sometimes even busier than during the legislative session."

It is not surprising that this challenging career has its ups and downs. Mark Takai describes his feelings about the job: "The period of nonsession months during the campaign season is really tough and grueling. And, including time spent at receptions, dinners, and so on, I probably spend about seventy hours a week working.

"However, the people I work with (both in the state capitol and throughout the community) make my job most rewarding. I would not trade the experiences that I have had for any other job. Although it can be very stressful and time-consuming, I truly enjoy my job as a state representative.

"I derive great pleasure from doing for others. For instance, one of my most rewarding moments occurred when I was able to provide assistance in getting funds to build a new traffic signal at an intersection that saw many near accidents, numerous accidents, and one fatality.

"The least enjoyable part of my job is knowing full well that every bill that we pass and that becomes law has a negative impact on someone or on a specific profession. Although I have voted for many bills that do much good for our community overall, sometimes it is these same bills that get people laid off from their jobs, and so forth. Knowing this causes me great pain."

Advice from the Professionals

The professionals we have met in this chapter have some advice for anyone considering a career in government or politics.

Karen Sweeny-Justice is honest about the realities of being a park ranger: "Working for the park service can be mentally draining, especially if you want to make it a career. I say this because it is very competitive, and there are no guarantees that permanent employment will come to you. I had to take a job as a permanent secretary to get my 'status' to apply for permanent ranger positions. And as a seasonal employee, you don't get any benefits, such as insurance, and you can be let go at any time.

"If you don't like speaking to total strangers or giving programs to audiences that range from a few people to crowds of more than a hundred, you wouldn't really enjoy this job. But for those of us who do—it's perfect!"

Vera Marie Badertscher offers this advice for aspiring campaign managers: "I would advise anyone interested in entering this kind of work to introduce yourself to a candidate you admire and volunteer to help. Political science classes teach theory, but only campaigning teaches campaigning. Don't try to tell the candidate how to run his or her campaign or volunteer to be the brains behind the organization until you have actually done some of the grunt work of campaigning and learned it from the inside out. You'd be surprised how many people come to a campaign manager and say, 'I'm really good at strategy,' when all the campaign manager really needs is someone to go out in a pickup truck and put up signs. And before any of that—register to vote. Read up on the issues. And last but not least—VOTE!"

Wade Hyde offers his view on how to prepare for campaign work: "I would advise others interested in entering this field to understand fully and honestly why you are working for a candidate. Know if you're primarily in it for a job, an appointment, for the experience and excitement, or for the candidate. Be realistic and don't hang around too long because burnout can set in quite soon. See *Wag the Dog* and *Primary Colors*—I found them to be pretty accurate as campaign compilations."

K. Mark Takai has some advice for those who want to run for public office: "I would encourage anyone interested in pursuing this kind of career to talk to people about what their concerns are. Meet with various leaders in your community. Get involved with political campaigns or volunteer or work for an elected official. And if you are truly serious, begin your plans for an eventual run for public office. Good luck!"

For Additional Information

Information on appointed positions in local government can be obtained from:

International City/County Management Association
777 North Capitol Street NE, Suite 500
Washington, DC 20002
www.icma.org

Additional information on careers in politics and government can be found at:

Democratic National Committee
Young Democrats of America
430 South Capitol Street SE
Washington, DC 20003
www.democrats.org

Republication National Committee
310 First Street SE
Washington, DC 20003
www.rnc.org

The Congressional Management Foundation
513 Capitol Court NE, Suite 300
Washington, DC 20002
www.cmfweb.org

United States Office of Personnel Management
1900 E Street NW
Washington, DC 20415
www.opm.gov

USAJOBS
www.usajobs.opm.gov

USAJOBS is the federal government's official source for federal jobs and employment information. Visitors to the website can search thousands of federal jobs, create and submit a resume, and download forms.

CHAPTER SIX

Careers on Foreign Soil

A man's feet should be planted in his country,
but his eyes should survey the world.
—George Santayana

On March 1, 1961, at a time when the Cold War between East and West raged and Germany stood divided, President Kennedy launched the Peace Corps. In the thirty-plus years since then, Peace Corps volunteers have maintained the same mission: providing volunteers to battle disease, poverty, hunger, and deprivation all over the globe and to teach people of other nations about America and Americans in order to promote world understanding. Since then, more than 140,000 Americans have served as Peace Corps volunteers. Today, 6,000 such individuals are performing their services in more than ninety countries in Asia, the Middle East, South and Central America, the Caribbean, the Pacific, Africa, and central Europe.

Foreign correspondents and foreign service officers are two other careers that offer opportunities for patriotic types to serve their country abroad.

Peace Corps Volunteers

Host countries make specific requests for individuals with particular expertise. Some of the skills most often requested include the areas of technical education, primary and secondary education, health and nutrition, natural resources, and agriculture. Volunteers are not asked simply to go over to these countries and do all the work. Their role is to serve as teachers or trainers by providing the necessary information, techniques, and expertise to the host country citizens so that they may become self-sufficient.

Qualifications and Training

Applicants for the Peace Corps must be United States citizens who are at least eighteen years of age (no limit on the upper end), healthy, free from financial debt, and willing to undergo an eight- to twelve-week training program in addition to a two-year service period. Workshops are held to reinforce skills and formulate and disseminate plans. Married couples without children are eligible as long as they meet all qualifications. It usually takes about ten months from the receipt of an application to the beginning of training. While you may indicate an area or areas you would prefer for assignment, this limits your possibilities for placement.

Most assignments require a minimum of a bachelor's degree. In some cases, an associate's degree along with a specified number of years of experience may suffice. Other jobs require a master's degree or three to five years of experience in lieu of or in addition to a college degree.

Volunteers receive transportation to and from their assignment locations and twenty-four days of vacation each year. Free medical and dental care are provided along with a monthly stipend to allow for housing, food, clothes, and other living expenses. Often student loan payments are deferred for the time period of the service. Upon fulfilling the service, volunteers are given a readjustment allowance of approximately $5,400 in addition to assistance in their job search. Some opt to take advantage of the available eligibility for federal employment on a noncompetitive basis. Also, many institutions offer special scholarships and assistantships for volunteers who return home.

Returning volunteers cite the following benefits of Peace Corps work: a way to see diverse parts of the world, an opportunity to get to know and be of help to people in Third World countries, a rewarding feeling, and, in many cases, substantial personal growth.

A Close-Up Look at the Peace Corps

Following are the personal accounts of five former Peace Corps volunteers. Perhaps their stories will strike a chord in you.

Kathleen Klug, Peace Corps Volunteer. Kathleen Klug learned about the Peace Corps through various social studies classes in high school. She had already developed an interest in other cultures and community service—interests that can be easily pursued in the Peace Corps. "I attended Peace Corps recruiting presentations at my university to obtain more specific information about becoming a volunteer," she says. "In the fall of my senior year, I submitted the lengthy Peace Corps application and interviewed with a recruiter. Speaking with the recruiter gave me a truer picture of the application process. I was told that it probably would be difficult to find a placement for me due to my nontechnical background. At that time (and now, too), the Peace Corps tried to recruit individuals with degrees or a background in subjects such as medicine, farming, horticulture, engineering, construction, physics/chemistry/math, Teaching English as a Second Language (TESL), and so forth. However, some of my course work and volunteer experience helped me to pass this first step of the application process. I graduated with a B.S. in psychology and political science. I also had my CPR/First Aid certification and some health education course work."

Klug kept in contact with her recruiter and waited four months until the second step of the process, when she received a nomination in the health nutrition extension. She then provided the required information for a full background check, including fingerprinting, and had a complete medical exam. The third step was an invitation to serve in the area of water/sanitation health education in Ghana, West Africa. It was eight months from the time Klug submitted her application until she left for Ghana.

The fourth step of the process, a five-day staging, took place in Chicago with other volunteers headed for the same host country. As Klug describes it, "The individuals in my training group were in their twenties and thirties, for the most part, and came from all over the United States. Staging is basically a time for people to get to know one another and gain general information about the Peace Corps and Ghana and so forth."

Klug then proceeded to the fifth step, traveling to her host country of Ghana. She began training at Mfantsipim Senior Secondary School in Cape Coast, Ghana. The intensive ten weeks included training in language (Fante and Twi), culture, and technical education, in addition to field experience. During the technical phase of the training, the volunteer group was divided into sections: education, water/sanitation health education, forestry, and business, depending on an individual's assignment. In Klug's water/sanitation health education section, she learned such things as latrine and well construction, health education (oral dehydration salts, waterborne diseases, and so on), and nonformal education methods.

"In September, I was happily sworn in as a U.S. Peace Corps Volunteer with approximately forty-six other new volunteers," she says. She was assigned to a site in the Kumasi region of the country in a medium-size village called Manso Nkwanta (the district capital). During the first few months of service, Klug spent most of her time meeting with people in the village and surrounding district villages and discussing and evaluating the water/sanitation health education needs. They also discussed plans to meet those needs and determined how Klug could help to facilitate the plans.

Working as a health educator, Klug reported to a fifteen-person Manso Nkwanta District Health and Sanitation Committee, the

Ministry of Community Development district officer, the district coordinator of the Ghana National Commission on Children, and three district health nurses.

Klug was able to achieve several goals during her assignment in Ghana. "My accomplishments include helping to organize a project committee from the existing district health committee for the construction of a ten-seater Kumasi Ventilated Improved Pit (KVIP) latrine in Manso Nkwanta. In working with the traditional village council, communal labor was organized to construct the latrine. The construction was complemented by a health education seminar on sanitation.

"Additionally, I worked with the community development district officer to initiate health and sanitation education and awareness in the district through presentations and informal discussions and spent time at the district clinic assisting the community health nurses with record keeping, baby weighing, immunizations, and nutritional counseling. I also began teaching English at the local junior secondary school as a secondary service project, following water/sanitation health education.

"During my service, I enjoyed traveling to other regions of Ghana as well as surrounding countries. Another factor that made my Peace Corps experience interesting is that I lived with the royal family in my village. Since ceremonies such as the swearing in of a chief often took place in the traditional district capital, Manso Nkwanta, I was able to attend most of these events. In particular, I saw many religious holiday celebrations that predominantly consisted of prayer and dancing."

Julia Harlan, Peace Corps Volunteer. Julia Harlan of Unionville, Indiana, is in the final year of her master's in public affairs program at Indiana University's School of Public and Environmental Affairs. Her specialized concentration is international development strategies. Harlan earned her undergraduate degree in 1988 at Barnard College, Columbia University, majoring in

American history. In 1991, she earned a law degree at the University of Wisconsin Law School. She is licensed to practice law in Tennessee and Wisconsin and will soon be sworn in to the New York state bar.

Julia Harlan served as a Peace Corps volunteer from June 1995 to September 1997. At the time of her application, she was working as an attorney for a private law firm. Although she was earning a good salary and enjoyed the challenging job, Harlan knew that working for a large firm wasn't the type of career she really wanted to pursue, and she decided that the time was right to make a change.

Harlan learned the importance of volunteering early in life, since her mother was involved in VISTA as both a volunteer and coordinator. She decided to commit herself to public service on a full-time basis. "I thought that I had the skills and education that would allow me to make a contribution," she says, "and I had the added benefit of not yet being married or owning any property, both of which require long-term commitments.

"Actually, I was not planning on joining the Peace Corps. I had hoped to become a VISTA volunteer. This was because of my mother's positive experience with the program and my belief that you don't have to leave the country to discover service opportunities. However, due to financial considerations, I decided to join the Peace Corps."

Harlan believes that working as an attorney provided valuable preparation for her time with the Peace Corps. As she says, "I had worked closely with my firm's business clients and was aware of some of the issues that face any entrepreneurs. Additionally, it helped me face situations with a diplomacy that was necessary when working in another culture. Finally, I was not overwhelmed by the amount of work I encountered, as I had come from a profession that requires major time commitments.

"Other experiences that helped me were my various kinds of volunteer service since high school. I came from a background that placed a great importance on public service. Although my father focused his energy on his job, his income afforded my mother the opportunity to serve on different boards and become very active in local activities. And at a young age, my brothers and I found ourselves working as volunteers for various organizations at a variety of events. I think I just have always assumed that since I had the good fortune to be provided with a number of advantages in life, I owe something back to society in general."

During her Peace Corps assignment in Latvia, Harlan's primary work sites were the regional government's Economic Development Office and the European Community's Entrepeneur Development Center. She also worked on other projects, including teaching business law and various development and training projects.

Harlan describes her duties: "Generally, I would try to help people or organizations to define issues or problems, develop a solution, and then implement this solution. Often I tried to find resources (people, training options, materials) that would benefit the client. I also became very involved in aspects of Peace Corps as an organization, serving on boards and training new volunteers."

Harlan enjoyed a comfortable standard of living while in the Peace Corps and describes the atmosphere of the offices where she worked as informal and relaxed. She generally worked a forty-hour week in the offices and spent additional time working on other projects and traveling to the capital city where she taught.

"I liked the freedom I had in accomplishing my work as a volunteer," she says. "Under some very general constraints, I was able to undertake a wide variety of projects that interested me and that were beneficial to my community in Latvia. I honestly feel that I was able to provide some help to the people I worked with during my time as a volunteer. And the most positive result of my experience was discovering my interest in continuing in development work. This led me to return to school for more training so that I could pursue a career in development."

Dina Siber-Jaco, Peace Corps Volunteer. Dina Siber-Jaco served in the Peace Corps in Albania. Prior to her service, she earned a bachelor of arts degree in international affairs from George Washington University in Washington, D.C. After her Peace Corps service, she earned a master's degree in regional planning from Cornell University in Ithaca, New York. She also worked as a development worker for Los Niños, a nonprofit group promoting self-sufficiency in low-income communities in Tijuana, Mexico. There she specialized in nutritional education for women and taught mathematics and Spanish grammar for adults working toward their elementary education diplomas.

Siber-Jaco had been interested in the Peace Corps for some time. "After researching many organizations and after my experience working for a small nonprofit group, I wanted to be part of an organization that had a greater influence in the country of service," she says. She was accepted into the Peace Corps in June 1992 and served as a member of the first program ever to be established in Albania, where she specialized in teaching English as a foreign language and in youth development programs.

"During my final year of college, I sent in three applications," she says. "The first was to a graduate program in economics, with a specialty in development economics and development ethics. The second went to a small nonprofit organization, Los Niños, and the third to the Peace Corps. I was accepted into the graduate program. Consequently, I visited the school, met with the professors, and made a decision that I was too young to go to graduate school and that I needed field experience before I could tackle the questions in graduate school. I was also accepted to Los Niños, but I was still waiting for an answer from the Peace Corps. Given the long application process and the series of interviews necessary, I knew I could work at Los Niños for a year and then move on to the Peace Corps. My timing was correct, and in May 1992 I ended my service with Los Niños and left for Albania in June 1992."

Siber-Jaco's previous employment was working as an economic research assistant at the Economic Research Service (U.S. Department of Agriculture) and the Office of the Comptroller (U.S. Department of the Treasury). She also held various internships at the Organization of American States (OAS); the United Nations Economic Commission on Latin America and the Caribbean (ECLAC); a New York publishing firm; a Washington, D.C., art gallery; and an arts magazine. At Los Niños, she was a development worker.

Siber-Jaco feels that her earlier experiences were good preparation for her work with the Peace Corps. "The most relevant experience was my work in Mexico, given that the conditions and the type of work was similar. I also felt that my other experiences were relevant since my Peace Corps experience was not limited only to English teaching. A component of the work was negotiating and finding sources of funding for new projects. For example, I was able to qualify for funding to purchase sports equipment for a girls' sports camp that some fellow teachers in the community and I started. In addition, a computer was donated to my school so that I was able teach an after-school computer course to interested students.

"Given that the Peace Corps had no experience or history in Albania, volunteers were given extra freedoms in starting new programs and customizing their projects to the needs of the community. Although I was assigned as an English teacher at a local high school, I started after-school programs targeted at female high school students."

While in Albania, Siber-Jaco lived in a predominantly Muslim town where the activities of women and girls were limited. Due to her position as the only foreigner and the only one her age, she was often approached for advice and information by the young women of the town, which led her to discover more ways in which she could help the community.

Siber-Jaco says, "In developing a relationship with the girls, I found that once school ended, their activities were limited to working in the home or watching television. As a young woman, I was also limited in what I could do. (Of course, I could have done what I wanted, but I needed to maintain a professional image in order to earn respect in the community.) Given my limitations, for example on exercise, I would run in the soccer stadium adjacent to my school. Many of my students would see me and ask if they could join me. In talking to them, I found out that many of them enjoyed basketball and volleyball, and, as a result, I organized after-school basketball and volleyball games for girls."

She describes a typical day in Albania:

8:30 A.M.—Daily gathering of teachers in the teachers' room, announcement for the day.

9:00 A.M.—Classes begin.

9:00 a.m. to 1:00 P.M.—Depending on the day, I would have three to four classes, each a forty-five-minute period.

1:30 to 2:00 P.M.—Daily run at the soccer stadium (weather permitting).

2:00 P.M.—Lunch at home or sometimes a visit to a colleague's home.

3:30 P.M.—Nap. Everyone in my host family would fall into a light afternoon nap after lunch. In my second year, I started a computer class for students (one hour).

4:00 to 8:00 P.M.—Weather permitting, I would play basketball with some of my students. In the winter, activities were limited to reading, preparing lessons for the next day, meeting visitors who came to my host family's home, or just talking.

8:00 P.M.—Dinner and the news.

9:00 P.M.—Reading, talking, and so forth.

Siber-Jaco talks about the ups and downs of her work with the Peace Corps. "The most interesting part of my work was the people I met and interacted with—my students, my host family, and the host of friends I made. Peace Corps work is not traditional in that it doesn't come to an end at 5 P.M. every day. The Peace Corps really is an experience and series of events and relationships. I enjoyed just being in the country and learning about the culture, the history, the language, and the current situation. My job as a teacher was only one small part of my experience. I felt that I was an outlet for people; I was someone who they could learn from and talk to, just as they were to me. We both exchanged parts of our cultures and who we were.

"Of course, there were difficult times. The most difficult was being able to do my job with extremely limited resources, if any, as well as feeling unprepared. As a volunteer, I was trained to teach intermediate-level students of English. When I arrived at my school, I was faced with classes of beginning-level students and some who had never even studied a day of English. Like all volunteers, I learned to deal with the situation and do the best that I could."

Kendra Spangler, Peace Corps Volunteer. Kendra Spangler served in the Peace Corps in Suceava, Romania, beginning in June 1997. She earned a bachelor of arts degree in Spanish at the State University at Albany, New York, in 1992. Her Peace Corps specialty was Teaching of English as a Foreign Language (TOEFL).

"Before entering the Peace Corps, I worked as an administrative assistant at the Abraham Fund, a nonprofit organization in New York City. I always had a romantic idea of what service in the Peace Corps would be like," Spangler says, "roughing it in the African wilderness, helping people, and so on. Although it isn't always like that, I knew that any experience would only broaden my own mind and give me a deeper understanding of the people with whom I was in contact. Besides, it seemed like the perfect time (after school) to join. I wanted the Peace Corps to give me the foundation for a career in the international field."

During her junior year of college, Spangler lived in Barcelona, Spain, an experience that helped prepare her for her time in Romania. "I really enjoyed the everyday interactions and the challenges I faced living in another culture," she says. "I found that being able to speak the language put me into another level with the people. I was more respected and more accepted—not just looked upon as a tourist. This experience gave me an edge when I arrived in Romania. I acquired the language quickly and had the facilities to adapt within the society."

In Romania, Spangler taught English to middle and high school students for sixteen hours each week. Her classes were focused on communication skills that are not generally applied in the regular English courses taught by Romanian teachers. In addition to language, Spangler taught her students about American culture and history. She also taught basic computer skills in English.

Spangler found the work rewarding and never felt any sense of danger in her host country. She was well respected by the students, and she established very positive relationships with her Romanian colleagues.

"As Peace Corps volunteers teaching English, we are required to have a secondary project," she says. "I chose to teach English in a small village that does not have an English program. It has been a tremendous experience for me. When I go, I stay with a Romanian family that has adopted me as their third daughter. With them, I have been able to truly experience the ways of the Romanian people.

"My favorite part of all of this is my interaction with the children. They are eager, enthusiastic, invigorating, and extremely bright. They are the ones who recharge my batteries, so to speak. On the other side of the spectrum, it has been difficult to adjust to the Romanian timetable. Things are resolved in Romania at a much slower pace than in the United States."

Cristyn Elder, Peace Corps Volunteer. Cristyn Elder earned a bachelor of arts degree in comparative literature with a concentration in Spanish from California State University, Long Beach, in 1993. She also has a master of arts in TESOL (Teaching English to

Speakers of Other Languages) from the Monterey Institute of International Studies in California. She is assistant professor of English for Academic and Professional Purposes and coordinator of Pre-Academic English Programs at the Monterey Institute.

Elder worked as an English as a Foreign Language (EFL) instructor in Morelia, Michoacán, Mexico, from 1993 to 1995, at La Universidad Latina de America and at high school campuses. She taught EFL and also served as an English language teacher trainer.

While pursuing her master's degree, Elder worked as a Peace Corps Master's Internationalist Volunteer in Ukraine. Master's Internationalists are those volunteers who join the Peace Corps after completing the first year of graduate school. Upon completing her Peace Corps tour of duty, she returned to graduate school to report on her work abroad as a volunteer and to finish her last semester of study. She served in Ukraine from June 1997 to July 1999.

Elder describes her initial work in Mexico: "In the summer of 1992, when I was a student at California State University, Long Beach, I went on a five-week study-abroad program to Morelia, Mexico. I truly enjoyed the time I spent in Mexico and knew I wanted to go back, so after graduating from college in Spring 1993, I moved to Morelia. Upon arriving, I opened up the newspaper to look for an apartment and went down the list of schools in the phone book and started calling each one. It wasn't long before I had three teaching jobs and was turning down more. I taught EFL classes at both a private university and high school as well as a private tutoring institute. I began teaching mainly because I knew it was something I could do to support myself while living in Mexico. It started out as a way to survive, but I quickly came to realize that not only was I good at it, I also really enjoyed my students and teaching. I even started developing my own teaching materials and conducted training workshops for my colleagues.

"Due to the decrease in the value of the peso and because I knew I wanted to go to graduate school, I decided to return to California in 1995. I decided to study TESOL because I was good at teaching and felt that being an EFL teacher was my ticket around the world. I could go just about anywhere and support myself through teaching. When I applied to the Monterey Institute of International Studies, I found out that they offered a degree in TESOL that could also be combined with serving as a Peace Corps volunteer." (Elder received four units toward her degree for serving in the Peace Corps, as well as a scholarship for her last eleven units.)

"My initial reason for joining the Peace Corps was that I wanted to share the education I received at Monterey with those who do not have access to the same educational opportunities. In addition, I saw learning a new language, learning about a new culture, and traveling as great benefits to the job."

During her assignment in Ukraine, Elder worked primarily in the Southern Ukraine Regional In-Service Teacher Training Institute in Kherson, where she taught teacher-development courses for Ukrainian English teachers. These courses were taught four times a year for three-week intervals. During the time between courses, Elder taught EFL at a secondary school for six hours each week. The rest of her time was devoted to various tasks, such as developing materials and conducting workshops and seminars in other cities.

Elder has written a teacher-training manual that describes her work in these courses. The manual is intended for use by less-experienced and less-educated EFL volunteers who will be working in teacher training. She has also completed a pilot project with Oxford University Press for a new textbook, *Open Doors*. In collaboration with a fellow volunteer, Elder is also working on an AIDS-education curriculum for secondary schools in Ukraine.

"I am a very fortunate volunteer in that my Ukrainian counterparts at both the training institute and the secondary school are very supportive and encourage me in all my projects." she says. "One reason I love teaching is because I am not required to work from nine to five (and, of course, I have great summer and winter vacations). The hours I spend at the secondary school and the teacher-training courses are really the only set schedule I have. The rest of the day (or month), I dictate how and on what projects my time will be spent.

"Also, I love working with students and other teachers. The students keep me young and let me know what is happening with the new generation. Also, because I am a teacher trainer, I am required to stay up-to-date with the latest theories and trends in teaching. Furthermore, my job is never the same on a day-to-day basis, and it provides me with a creative outlet.

"What I like least about my job is that I can never stop thinking about what I have to plan for tomorrow. Also, unlike some jobs, I have to take my work home with me every night—whether it's to correct students' papers or to plan for the next day. I'm also disappointed that teaching is not seen as a more prestigious profession. I think many people in society don't realize what an influence teachers have on their children, the next generation. Teachers not only teach their subjects but also teach cultural values and help students develop their social skills. Sadly enough, teachers often spend more time raising other people's children for them. What is even worse is that it is often said that the best teachers are usually the first ones to quit teaching."

Advice from the Professionals

The five women we have just met all have advice for anyone who is considering becoming a Peace Corps volunteer.

Kathleen Klug says: "The best advice I can give to a potential Peace Corps volunteer is to be patient and flexible during the whole process. Some individuals have very high or very specific expectations, and those are generally the people who quit prior to their close of service."

But those who, like Klug, maintain the right attitude echo the Peace Corps slogan: "The toughest job you'll ever love."

Julia Harlan offers these words: "I would advise others who are looking to serve their country to consider why they are joining the Peace Corps and what they look to get out of the experience. It seems to me that people who joined to 'save the world' were either oblivious to their underlying agendas or were trying to escape something. I think you can contribute as a volunteer but that it helps to have a micro instead of a macro viewpoint on what you can accomplish in just two years. One of my primary motivations to join was to help, but I also wanted to benefit from the experience. It was a good opportunity to learn new skills and experience a new perspective. I also hope that I accomplished some good."

Dina Siber-Jaco reflects on the rewards of volunteering: "If the Peace Corps is something you always wanted to do, then do it. Times can get difficult, so you really have to believe in your work and what you are doing. Although some people dwell on the time commitment, it is two years that you will never forget and one of the best experiences you will ever have."

Kendra Spangler avidly promotes Peace Corps work: "I would advise anyone who has an interest in serving in the Peace Corps to definitely try it. Every single experience is different from the next. There are surprises and disappointments, successes and frustrations, but, on the whole, it will be an experience one could never forget."

Cristyn Elder offers advice for those considering a career like hers: "Following in my footsteps may mean one of two things—becoming an EFL teacher and/or a Peace Corps volunteer. In either case, I would suggest that you ask a teacher in a local school or college if you could observe some classes and even take time to interview different teachers about the profession. Finally, I would recommend volunteering as a teacher's aide or as an English language teacher at a local church or a nonprofit literacy organization to test out whether you might enjoy teaching.

"However, be forewarned. Just because you may find you don't enjoy teaching primary students or adults, for example, it doesn't mean you wouldn't enjoy teaching high school kids or international university students."

Foreign Correspondents

In an effort to keep the country up-to-date on all the newsworthy events abroad, foreign correspondents are employed by networks, news services, television or radio stations, and major magazines or newspapers. They may also operate as freelance agents.

Acting as reporters, foreign correspondents are sent overseas to various countries where they are responsible for tracking down and uncovering information via news conferences, research, private sources, wire services, interviews, and any other means they can devise. Once they obtain their information, they organize it and write articles and reports that are clear, concise, and well written for their audiences in the United States or their "home" country.

Working Conditions

Since newsworthy events may occur at any time, foreign correspondents hardly work nine to five. Many breaking news events are also potentially dangerous, so risk of injury or even death may also be part of the job.

Qualifications and Training

Most employers prefer that foreign correspondents have a bachelor's degree in journalism or mass communications or possibly a liberal arts degree with a strong background and experience in journalism.

Bachelor's degree programs in journalism are available at more than four hundred colleges and universities. About three-fourths of the courses in a typical curriculum are in the liberal arts; the remaining courses are in journalism. Examples of journalism courses are Introductory Mass Media, Basic Reporting, Copyediting, History of Journalism, and Press Law and Ethics. Those planning newspaper or magazine careers usually specialize in news-editorial journalism.

Correspondents need strong computer and word processing skills, outstanding written and oral communication skills, a "nose for news," and an ability to handle difficult situations. Knowing how to use computer software to combine story text with audio and video elements and graphics is essential for creating a news story for an online or broadcast presentation. Curiosity, research skills, persistence, patience, fortitude, honesty, and good people skills are also desirable qualities.

You can expect serious competition for foreign correspondent positions—only reporters with extensive experience will be given the opportunity to function as foreign correspondents.

Salaries

Depending on the employer, the location, and the correspondent's previous experience, salaries can range from around $30,000 to $75,000 or more.

A Close-Up Look at the Profession

What follows is a firsthand account from a veteran foreign correspondent. Does his career interest you?

Jerry King, Foreign Correspondent. "Originally, my desire was to pursue a career in education," says Jerry King, a foreign correspondent for ABC-TV for more than fifteen years. "I was planning to teach physical education, an area I always enjoyed. So I spent one year at the university in Canada but unfortunately didn't do well in chemistry and physics. Since these were both requirements for my major, I was afraid I might be taking those classes every year forever."

Realizing that he needed to refine his career goals, King became involved in broadcasting and sports reporting, particularly hockey, in Canada. He moved to Bermuda and spent a summer working as a radio DJ and reporting television news and sports, and then he moved to England and worked in the radio/audio division of United Press International.

King worked as a freelance radio journalist for ABC radio and as a correspondent in Germany. In 1975 he traveled to Beirut, where he worked for more than five years before returning to the United States. He was then offered a job overseas and returned to Germany to report on turmoil in Berlin.

"As a foreign correspondent, you have to be able to function in a variety of circumstances," King stresses. "During my career, I've been assigned to Northern Ireland, Vietnam, Lebanon, Afghanistan, Somalia, Iran, Iraq—the list goes on and on. In these situations, you have to exist without the creature comforts of home and also be creative and quick thinking. I've been in Beirut cut off from all outside contact for weeks on end—without telephones or any other form of communication. When we filmed scenes, we sometimes shot them with two cameras, hoping that at least one roll of film would make it out of the country."

King stresses the importance of working with local reporters. As he explains, "When I was living in Germany, for example, when Helmut Kohl wanted to say or do something, he didn't exactly call me up; his people called up the local reporters and got the word out through them. Maybe afterwards I could go back and get a particular slant or ask some specific questions, but my original information came from other journalists. The only exception is if you're on the spot of a breaking story, a hijacking for instance, where you can observe firsthand what is happening. I was lucky—in Poland I had a translator, a secretary, who knew Lech Walesa personally, so we had more access to him than some of the other journalists. I also had a cameraman in Lebanon who, on Christmas day, went around taking cookies to all the soldiers in the front lines because he wanted to make them his friends. He once told me that if you were caught someplace with a group of 'bad people,' you should always shake hands and keep shaking hands because they don't like to shoot you when they're shaking hands."

Working as a foreign correspondent can thrust one into an entirely different world, King says. "At one point, I was the first network television correspondent to come out of Warsaw after martial law was declared. We had been cut off so securely there from outside contact that the only thing we could hear was the BBC World Service shortwave broadcast. As time marched on, I thought the world had lost interest in the story because the situation had not changed much. But when I was suddenly able to make my way out of the country by train, I was amazed at how much interest there actually was. ABC quickly flew me to London, arranged for me to board a Concord headed for New York, and the next day I appeared on 'This Week with David Brinkley,' 'Good Morning America,' and 'Sunday Morning.'

"I've seen humanity at its best and at its worst," Jerry King says. "As a foreign correspondent, you are allowed to meet some pretty interesting people and witness some really fascinating things. On the other hand, there's also a tremendous boredom factor sitting around in places like Baghdad where you're not allowed to do anything but wait. Getting through those days was not easy. And there are many times when you put in long hours researching, interviewing, writing, and rewriting your stories. Though being a foreign correspondent certainly involves hard work, it is incredibly enjoyable."

Foreign Service Careers

Working for the U.S. Department of State, Foreign Service officers (FSOs) advocate American foreign policy, protect American citizens, and promote American business interests throughout the world. They staff embassies, consulates, and other diplomatic missions. The Foreign Service has five different career tracks: Management Affairs, Consular Affairs, Economic Affairs, Political Affairs, and Public Diplomacy.

Qualifications and Training

Many Foreign Service officers have degrees in liberal arts or business. Some FSOs hold advanced degrees in specialized areas ranging from law to the social and hard sciences. Knowledge of a foreign language is not a requirement to join the Foreign Service because language training is provided for overseas assignments. However, the U.S. Department of State welcomes applicants who have foreign language competence, especially in Slavic, Middle Eastern, and Asian languages.

After an initial orientation and training period in Washington (usually between three months and one year), newly hired FSOs are assigned overseas. During their first two assignments (each lasting two years), officers hold a variety of positions in order to demonstrate their qualifications for tenure as career Foreign Service officers. As part of this process, newly hired officers perform at least one year of consular work overseas and are frequently assigned to at least one hardship post.

Job Settings

Foreign Service officers serve in Washington, D.C., and at 265 diplomatic posts around the world. FSOs work in Africa; North, Central, and South America; East Asia and the Pacific; Europe and Eurasia; the Middle East and North Africa; and South Asia.

Some locations are designated as hardship posts. These are situations where the living conditions are considered more difficult than in the United States. Such factors as climate, the quality of local health care, crime rate, pollution levels, and availability of spouse employment opportunities are used in deciding which posts are given a hardship designation. Generally, most locations outside of Western Europe, Canada, and Australia are considered hardship posts. Employees serving at such posts receive a hardship differential of between 5 and 25 percent of salary, depending on the severity of the hardship. For example, in 2003, Asunción, Paraguay, was a 5 percent hardship differential post; Bucharest, Romania, was a 15 percent post; and Kigali, Rwanda, was a 25 percent post.

Assignments are made based on a bidding process. Employees submit a list of desired assignments from a list of current openings. After close consultation with the employee, the Bureau of Human Resources then selects an appropriate posting. Personal as well as professional factors are taken into account in making assignments, but the needs of the service remain paramount.

Salaries for Foreign Service Officers

Entry salaries for Foreign Service officers are determined through a two-part process. Part one determines the employee's grade and step based on education and/or experience levels. In 2004, a newly hired FSO with a bachelor's degree and no professional experience, or with no degree and six or fewer years' professional experience, earned $36,929. Salary is increased by increments, or steps, for additional experience. For example, a candidate with a bachelor's degree plus five years of professional experience earned $42,811; the same salary applied to a candidate with no degree and eleven years of professional experience.

A candidate with a master's degree or law degree, or with a bachelor's degree and six years of professional experience, earned $41,310. The same salary was earned by a candidate with no college degree and a minimum of twelve years of experience.

A candidate with a doctorate and no professional experience earned $50,981. This is the same salary earned by those with a master's or law degree and six years' professional experience, or a bachelor's degree and twelve years' experience, or no college degree and minimum of eighteen years' experience.

Part two of the salary determination process is an attempt to match salaries for employees who would lose money by joining the Foreign Service. Based on education and experience, if it is determined that the candidate will earn less as an FSO than in previous employment, the starting salary is raised to the step in grade that is closest to his or her current salary.

In addition to salary, FSOs are eligible for health benefits, savings and investments plans, and life insurance. They may also be eligible for partial repayment of student loans.

A Close-Up Look at the Profession

Following is the personal account of a former Foreign Service officer. Perhaps her story will awaken your interest in this career.

Geraldine Mosher, Foreign Service Careerist. Geraldine Mosher earned a B.A. from the University of Michigan at Ann Arbor with a major in English literature. She worked for the Department of State for twenty years as a communications and records clerk. During her career, Mosher was assigned to Washington, D.C.; Port-au-Prince, Haiti; Port of Spain, Trinidad; La Paz, Bolivia; Bonn, Germany; Belgrade, Yugoslavia; Recife, Brazil; Brasília, Brazil; Helsinki, Finland; Dakar, Senegal; and Guatemala City, Guatemala.

"My interest in doing this kind of work was sparked while at the University of Michigan, where I met and associated with many foreign students," Mosher says. "I was interested in getting a job that allowed me to work overseas and to travel. I was inspired to work for the government because of President Kennedy.

"Also, my father was a World War I veteran and my mother was active in the American Legion Auxiliary, which provided me with one of the scholarships that I needed in order to go to college. I have always been very patriotic and, therefore, it was understandable that I would go to work for the government."

Although working in the communications field at foreign posts was challenging and demanding, Mosher appreciated the importance of her job. She says, "It is, however, a vital job and gave me a feeling that what I was doing was important—that I was needed.

My job involved all forms of communication and records—radio, telegraph, encryption, telephone, mail, diplomatic courier, filing, and so forth."

At large posts, Mosher worked in shifts. Generally, she worked two weeks on the day shift (8 A.M. to 4 P.M.), two weeks on the swing shift (4 P.M. to midnight) and two weeks on "mids" (midnight to 8 A.M.). The shift work often made it difficult to socialize, since days off often fell during the week, rather than on weekends.

At other posts, Mosher worked days only (from 7 A.M. to 6 or 7 P.M.) and worked half days on Saturday on a rotating basis. She was also required to stand duty on a rotating basis, which meant being on call around the clock. This was often challenging in underdeveloped countries that had unreliable communications service.

"Work was usually busy (sometimes hectic). In case of any emergencies (uprising, coup d'état, flood, VIP visits, and so on), the communicators all worked throughout until the emergency was over," Mosher says.

"Some places where I worked were very dangerous because of shootings, embassy bombings, and kidnappings. Others were very dangerous because of conditions that could severely affect health, such as malaria, plague, extremely high altitude, or bad water."

Geraldine Mosher talks about her likes and dislikes on the job. "What I liked most about my career in the Foreign Service was, one, the feeling that my job was vital and, two, the social life (because of transfers, one was accepted and invited immediately upon arrival, and friendships were formed quickly). I also liked being able to travel, seeing different places, and getting to know (and hopefully understand) other cultures.

"What I liked least about foreign service was the stress that I had to work under—stress caused by political upheavals and stress caused by close living and working conditions—not being able to really 'get away' from the job.

"I would advise anyone wanting to follow in my footsteps simply to go for it! Working for the Foreign Service is wonderful, challenging, and fulfilling. Working overseas is very educational and makes you realize how great our country really is."

For Additional Information

The Peace Corps website is a good place to start gathering information for joining this international endeavor. Visit the site at: www.peacecorps.gov.

For information on a career as a foreign correspondent, look for the following guide in the local library or write to:

Journalism Career and Scholarship Guide
Dow Jones Newspaper Fund
PO Box 300
Princeton, NJ 08543
http://djnewspaperfund.dowjones.com/fund/default.asp

To learn more about careers in the Foreign Service, visit the website of the U.S. Department of State at www.careers.state.gov /officer.

CHAPTER SEVEN

Careers in Space

My country is the world, and my religion is to do good.
—Thomas Paine

For those patriotic types who also have a real sense of adventure, there are career options that exist outside the usual work environments; indeed, these careers involve work off the very ground. In this chapter we will consider the careers of air traffic controllers, air marshals, and astronauts.

Air Traffic Controllers

The air traffic control system is a vast network of people and equipment that ensures the safe operation of commercial and private aircraft. Air traffic controllers coordinate the movement of air traffic to make certain that planes stay a safe distance apart. Their immediate concern is safety, but controllers also must direct planes efficiently to minimize delays. Some regulate airport traffic; others regulate flights between airports.

Although controllers in airport towers and terminals watch over all planes traveling through an airport's airspace, their main responsibility is to organize the flow of aircraft into and out of the airport. Relying on radar and visual observation, they closely monitor each plane to ensure a safe distance between all aircraft and to guide pilots between the hangar or ramp and the end of the airport's airspace. In addition, controllers keep pilots informed about changes in weather conditions that can affect a flight.

Several controllers direct each plane during both arrival and departure. As a plane approaches an airport, the pilot radios ahead to inform the terminal of the plane's presence. The controller in the radar room, just beneath the control tower, has a copy of the plane's flight plan and has already observed the plane on radar. If the path is clear, the controller directs the pilot to a runway; if the airport is busy, the plane is fitted into a traffic pattern with other aircraft waiting to land. As the plane nears the runway, the pilot is asked to contact the tower. Another controller, who also is watching the plane on radar in the tower, monitors the aircraft the last mile or so to the runway, delaying any departures that would interfere with the plane's landing. Once the plane has landed, a ground controller in the tower directs it along the taxiways to its assigned gate. The ground controller usually works entirely by sight but may use radar if visibility is very poor.

This procedure is reversed for departures. The ground controller directs the plane to the proper runway. The local controller then informs the pilot about conditions at the airport, such as weather, speed and direction of wind, and visibility. The local controller also issues runway clearance for the pilot to take off. Once in the air, the plane is guided out of the airport's airspace by the departure controller.

After each plane departs, airport tower controllers notify the enroute controllers, who will next take charge. There are twenty-one enroute air traffic control centers located around the country, each employing 300 to 700 controllers, with more than 150 on duty during peak hours at the busier facilities. Airplanes usually fly along designated routes, and each center is assigned a certain airspace containing many different routes. Enroute controllers work in teams of up to three members, depending on how heavy traffic is; each team is responsible for a section of the center's airspace. For example, one team might be responsible for all planes that are between thirty and one hundred miles north of an airport and flying at an altitude between six thousand and eighteen thousand feet.

To prepare for planes about to enter the team's airspace, the radar associate controller organizes flight plans coming off a printer. If two planes are scheduled to enter the team's airspace at nearly the same time, location, and altitude, this controller may arrange with the preceding control unit for one plane to change its flight path. The previous unit may have been another team at the same or an adjacent center, or a departure controller at a neighboring terminal. As a plane approaches a team's airspace, the radar controller accepts responsibility for the plane from the previous controlling unit. The controller also delegates responsibility for the plane to the next controlling unit when the plane leaves the team's airspace.

The radar controller, who is the senior team member, observes the planes in the team's airspace on radar and communicates with the pilots when necessary. Radar controllers warn pilots about nearby planes, bad weather conditions, and other potential hazards. Two planes on a collision course will be directed around each other. If a pilot wants to change altitude in search of better flying conditions, the controller will check to determine that no other planes will be along the proposed path. As the flight progresses, the responsible team notifies the next team in charge of the airspace ahead. Through team coordination, the plane arrives safely at its destination.

Both airport tower and enroute controllers usually control several planes at a time; often, they have to make quick decisions about completely different activities. For example, a controller might direct a plane on its landing approach and at the same time provide pilots entering the airport's airspace with information about conditions at the airport. While instructing these pilots, the controller also would observe other planes in the vicinity, such as those in a holding pattern waiting for permission to land, to ensure that they remain well separated.

In addition to airport towers and enroute centers, air traffic controllers also work in flight service stations operated at more than a hundred locations. These flight service specialists provide pilots with information on the station's particular area, including terrain, preflight and inflight weather information, suggested routes, and other information important to the safety of a flight. Flight service station specialists help pilots in emergency situations and initiate and coordinate searches for missing or overdue aircraft. However, they are not involved in actively managing air traffic.

Some air traffic controllers are employed at the Federal Aviation Administration (FAA) Air Traffic Control Systems Command Center in Herndon, Virginia, where they oversee the entire system. They look for situations that will create bottlenecks or other problems in the system and then respond with a management plan for traffic into and out of the troubled sector. The objective is to keep traffic levels in the trouble spots manageable for the controllers working at enroute centers.

The FAA is currently implementing a new automated air traffic control system, called the National Airspace System (NAS) Architecture. The NAS Architecture is a long-term strategic plan that will allow controllers to more efficiently deal with the demands of increased air traffic. It encompasses the replacement of aging equipment and the introduction of new systems, technologies, and procedures to enhance safety and security and support future aviation growth.

Working Conditions

Air traffic controllers work a basic forty-hour week; however, they may work additional hours for which they receive overtime pay or equal time off. Because most control towers and centers operate twenty-four hours a day, seven days a week, controllers rotate night and weekend shifts.

During busy times, controllers must work rapidly and efficiently. Total concentration is required to keep track of several planes at the same time and to make certain that all pilots receive correct instructions. The mental stress of being responsible for the safety of several aircraft and their passengers can be exhausting for some people.

Qualifications and Training

Enrollment in an FAA-approved education program is a requirement for working as an air traffic controller. In addition, one must pass a preemployment test that measures the ability to learn the controller's duties in order to qualify for job openings in the air traffic control system. Exceptions are military veterans and those air traffic controllers who have prior experience.

The preemployment test is currently offered only to students in the FAA Air Traffic Collegiate Training Initiative (AT-CTI) Program or the Minneapolis Community and Technical College, Air Traffic Control Training Program. In addition, applicants must have three years of full-time work experience or four years of college, or a combination of both. In combining education and experience, one year of undergraduate study (thirty semester or forty-five quarter hours) is equivalent to nine months of work experience.

Upon successful completion of an FAA-approved program, individuals who receive a school recommendation and who meet the basic qualification requirements, including age limit and achievement of a qualifying score on the FAA authorized preemployment test, become eligible for employment as air traffic controllers. Candidates also must pass a medical exam, drug screening, and security clearance before they can be hired.

New employees attend the FAA Academy in Oklahoma City for twelve weeks of additional training, during which they learn the fundamentals of the airway system, FAA regulations, controller equipment, and aircraft performance characteristics, as well as more specialized tasks.

After graduation, it takes several years of progressively more responsible work experience, interspersed with considerable classroom instruction and independent study, to become a fully qualified controller. Controllers who fail to complete either the academy or the on-the-job training are usually dismissed.

Controllers must pass a physical examination each year and a job performance examination twice each year. Failure to become certified in any position at a facility within a specified time also may result in dismissal. Controllers also are subject to drug screening as a condition of continuing employment.

Air traffic controllers must be articulate because pilots must be given directions quickly and clearly. Intelligence and a good memory also are important because controllers constantly receive information that they must immediately grasp, interpret, and remember. Decisiveness is also required because controllers often have to make quick decisions. The ability to concentrate is crucial because controllers must make these decisions in the midst of noise and other distractions.

At airports, new controllers begin by supplying pilots with basic flight data and airport information. They then advance to the position of ground controller, then local controller, departure controller, and, finally, arrival controller. At an air route traffic control center, new controllers first deliver printed flight plans to teams, gradually advancing to radar associate controller and then radar controller.

Controllers can transfer to jobs at different locations or advance to supervisory positions, including management jobs in air traffic control and top administrative jobs in the FAA. However, there are limited opportunities for controllers to switch from an enroute center to a tower.

Career Outlook

Employment of air traffic controllers is expected to grow about 10 to 20 percent through the year 2012. Increasing air traffic will require more controllers to handle the additional work. However, employment growth is not expected to keep pace with growth in the number of aircraft flying. New computerized systems will assist the controllers by automatically making many of the routine decisions. This will allow controllers to handle more traffic, thus increasing their productivity. Federal budget constraints also may limit hiring of air traffic controllers.

More job openings are expected due to replacement needs. The majority of today's air traffic controllers will be eligible to retire over the next decade, although not all are expected to do so. Nevertheless, replacement needs will be substantial and will result in hundreds of job opportunities each year for those graduating from the FAA training programs. Despite the increasing number of jobs coming open, competition to get into the FAA training programs is expected to remain keen, as there generally are many more applicants to get into the schools than there are openings. But those who graduate have good prospects of getting a job as a controller.

Air traffic controllers who continue to meet the proficiency and medical requirements enjoy more job security than do most workers. The demand for air travel and the workloads of air traffic controllers decline during recessions, but controllers seldom are laid off.

Salaries for Air Traffic Controllers

Median annual earnings of air traffic controllers in 2002 were $91,600. The middle 50 percent earned between $65,480 and $112,550. The lowest 10 percent earned less than $46,410, and the highest 10 percent earned more than $131,610.

The federal government employs 90 percent of air traffic controllers in the United States. In 2002, the average annual salary for these workers, excluding overtime earnings, in nonsupervisory, supervisory, and managerial positions, was $95,700. Both the worker's job responsibilities and the complexity of the particular facility determine a controller's pay. For example, controllers who work at the FAA's busiest air traffic control facilities earn higher salaries.

Depending on length of service, air traffic controllers receive thirteen to twenty-six days of paid vacation and thirteen days of paid sick leave each year, as well as life insurance and health benefits. In addition, controllers can retire at an earlier age and with fewer years of service than other federal employees. Air traffic controllers are eligible to retire at age fifty with twenty years of active service or after twenty-five years of active service at any age. There is a mandatory retirement age of fifty-six for controllers who manage air traffic. However, federal law provides for exemptions to the mandatory age of fifty-six, up to age sixty-one, for controllers with exceptional skills and experience.

Federal Air Marshals

According to the Department of Homeland Security, the mission of the Federal Air Marshal Service is "to be responsible for and protect air security and promote public confidence in our nation's civil aviation system through the effective deployment of Federal Air Marshals in order to detect, deter, and defeat hostile acts targeting U.S. air carriers, airports, passengers, and crews."

On September 11, 2001, the Federal Air Marshal Service (FAMS) employed thirty-three marshals. President George W. Bush authorized an increase in the number of air marshals, and the service immediately received more than two hundred thousand applications for employment. A classified number of applicants were screened, hired, trained, certified, and deployed on flights around the world. Today the Federal Air Marshal Service is a key component of the Immigration and Customs Enforcement Bureau, which serves as the largest investigative arm of the Department of Homeland Security in the war against terrorism.

Working Conditions

Federal air marshals must make split-second decisions at thirty thousand feet. They often work without backup and rely on their own training and instincts to make these life-and-death decisions while defending hundreds of lives. Air marshals must blend in with flight passengers yet remain constantly alert and vigilant.

Qualifications and Training

Candidates for the Federal Air Marshal Service must be United States citizens under thirty-seven years of age. Candidates cannot be initially appointed to covered federal law enforcement officer positions on or after their thirty-seventh birthday. Previous experience in a covered federal law enforcement position may exempt candidates from the age requirement.

Every federal air marshal candidate must successfully complete a two-phase training program to fulfill the requirements necessary to become a federal air marshal (FAM). The initial phase consists of a seven-week basic law enforcement officer training program conducted at the Federal Law Enforcement Training Center (FLETC) in Artesia, New Mexico. The FAM basic training has been specifically tailored to prepare recruits for the unique and critical mission of the Federal Air Marshal Service. The core curriculum taught during FAM basic training is drawn from the following disciplines: constitutional law, basic marksmanship, physical fitness, defensive tactics, emergency medical care, and basic law enforcement investigative and administrative practices. FAM candidates who successfully complete the basic training curriculum continue to Phase II training conducted at the Federal Air Marshal Training Center in Atlantic City, New Jersey.

Phase II training is dedicated to providing FAM candidates with the knowledge, skills, and abilities specifically applicable to the environment in which they will perform their duties. Emphasis is placed on developing proficiency in advanced firearms and defensive techniques, advanced operational tactics, strength conditioning and aerobic training, aircraft systems emergency procedures, and legal and administrative protocols. Candidates who successfully complete Phase II have demonstrated the ability to carry out the duties and tasks necessary to fulfill the mission of the Federal Air Marshal Service. Upon graduation from Phase II, newly appointed federal air marshals are assigned to one of the twenty-one field offices to begin flying missions.

Job Settings

Federal air marshals travel extensively on a regular basis. They are assigned to both foreign and domestic locations for several weeks at a time, work irregular hours and shifts, and are on twenty-four-hour call.

While deployed on an assignment, FAMs have limited contact with family and limited time off. Assignments can include countries that are politically or economically unstable and may pose a high probability of terrorist or criminal activity against the U.S. government. In addition, some locations may present health hazards such as poor sanitation and unsafe water.

Salaries for Federal Air Marshals

The basic salary range for federal air marshals is from $35,100 to $80,800. The salary range for each pay scale is as follows: level G, $35,100 to $54,300; level H, $42,800 to $66,200; and level I, $52,200 to $80,800.

In addition to base salary, FAM positions are covered by the 25 percent Law Enforcement Availability Pay (LEAP), which can substantially increase an employee's annual income. Salary is also adjusted to include locality pay based on the duty location of the position.

Astronauts

The space age began in the United States with the establishment of the National Aeronautics and Space Administration (NASA) in 1957. Created as a response to the launch of *Sputnik I* by the Soviet Union, the agency saw its first goal realized in 1969, when Neil

Armstrong landed on the moon. Space flights became almost routine until the near tragedy of *Apollo 13* and the deaths of the astronauts aboard the *Challenger* and *Columbia* space shuttles reminded all of us how dangerous space travel can be.

A host of people are needed in varying capacities in order to maintain the space program. Perhaps the best-known are those at the center of the program—our heroes, the astronauts.

Though the word *astronaut* means sailor among the stars, astronauts actually spend most of their time on the ground, preparing themselves to learn how to operate in space and gain knowledge of new horizons.

Astronaut Designations

Once astronauts are chosen and assigned to missions, they take their places as part of space shuttle crews that consist of at least five people: the commander, the pilot, and three mission specialists, all of whom are NASA astronauts. Some flights also call for payload specialists. Some crews also include engineers, technicians, physicians, meteorologists, or biologists. Crew members are trained and cross trained so that each can handle at least one other associate's duties, if necessary.

Pilot Astronauts. Pilot astronauts play a key role in space shuttle flights, serving as either commanders or pilots. During flights, commanders are responsible for the vehicle, the crew, mission success, and safety—duties analogous to those of the captain of a ship. Shuttle commanders are assisted by pilot astronauts, who are second in command and whose primary responsibilities involve controlling and operating the shuttle. During flights, commanders and pilots usually assist in spacecraft deployment and retrieval operations.

Mission Specialist Astronauts. Mission specialist astronauts, working closely with the commander and pilot, are responsible for coordinating onboard operations involving crew activity planning, use and monitoring of the shuttle's consumables (fuel, water, food, and so forth), and conducting experiment and payload activities. They are required to have a detailed knowledge of both the shuttle systems and the objectives and requirements of any experiments to be conducted on the mission. Mission specialists perform onboard experiments, spacewalks (extravehicular activity, or EVA), and payload-handling functions.

Payload Specialists. This newest category of shuttle crew member, the payload specialist, is a professional in the physical or life sciences or a technician skilled in operating equipment unique to the space shuttle mission. Selection of a payload specialist for a particular mission is made by the payload sponsor or customer. For NASA-sponsored spacecraft or experiments requiring a payload specialist, the specialist is nominated by an investigator working group and approved by NASA.

Qualifications and Training

At the high school level, it is important for potential candidates to earn high marks and score well on standardized tests (SAT and/or ACT). The minimum degree requirement for candidates is a bachelor's degree from an accredited institution.

The science departments of colleges and universities offer many degree options for students interested in careers in space. NASA provides funding for certain programs designed for those interested in the space program. See the next section on Space Grant Consortia for details.

Astronauts come from both military and civilian backgrounds. NASA accepts applications from qualified individuals on a continuing basis. Selected candidates participate in a rigorous one-year training program administered by the Johnson Space Center in Houston, Texas. Candidates who successfully complete the training program become regular members of the astronaut corps and are generally eligible for a flight assignment one year after completing the basic training program.

Pilot astronauts must have a bachelor's degree in engineering, biological science, physical science, or mathematics. A graduate degree is not a requirement but is preferred. Pilot candidates must have accumulated at least one thousand hours of flying time in jet aircraft. Experience as a test pilot is desirable, although it is not required.

Mission specialist candidates must have a bachelor's degree in engineering, biological science, physical science, or mathematics and at least three years of related and progressively responsible professional experience. An advanced degree can be substituted for all or part of the experience requirement (one year for a master's degree and three years for a doctorate).

All astronaut candidates must also pass a strict physical examination and meet requirements for vision, blood pressure, and height.

Initial training for new candidates consists of a series of short courses in aircraft safety—including instruction in ejection, parachute, and survival—to prepare them in the event their aircraft is disabled and they have to eject or make an emergency landing. Pilot and mission specialist astronauts are trained to fly T-38 high-performance jet aircraft, which allows pilots to maintain their flying skills and mission specialists to become familiar with high-performance jets.

In the formal academic areas, newly selected candidates are given a full range of basic science and technical courses, including mathematics, earth resources, meteorology, guidance and navigation, astronomy, physics, and computer sciences. Basic knowledge of the shuttle system, including payloads, is obtained through lectures, briefings, textbooks, and flight-operations manuals.

As training progresses, the student astronauts gain one-on-one experience in the single systems trainers (SSTs) at the Johnson Space Center (JSC). The SSTs contain computer databases with software that allows students to interact with controls and displays like those of a shuttle crew station. Here they can develop work procedures and react to malfunction situations in a shuttle-like environment. Learning to function in a weightless environment is simulated in aircraft and in an enormous neutral-buoyancy water tank at JSC.

NASA Space Grant Consortia

Space Grant supports both graduate and undergraduate students through a network of fifty-two university-based consortia in all fifty states, the District of Columbia, and Puerto Rico. In 2001, the network involved 820 affiliates, including 530 academic institutions. Each consortium receives fellowship (for graduate students) and scholarship (for undergraduates) funds from NASA. Most consortia supplement their NASA contributions with state or university funds. The consortia then distribute those funds competitively to student applicants from their member institutions.

In 2001, Space Grant awarded more than twenty-three hundred tuition-assistance awards averaging about $4,000. Undergraduate awards averaged $2,000 and graduate fellowships over $10,000. Awards are competitive at the state level, and each consortium has a different set of criteria for selection.

Most Space Grant awards include a mentored research experience with university faculty or NASA personnel. Summer internships and academic year internships are often available. Fields of study vary widely among the consortia. Subjects range from precollege science teaching to intricate graduate-level engineering design projects. Many of the Space Grant research projects involve collaboration among other students, faculty, and NASA scientists or engineers. Space Grant encourages all of the consortia to ensure that awardees participate in research, especially undergraduates.

For a complete list of which institutions, by state, are members of the Space Grant network, consult the Space Grant Contact Database: http://calspace.ucsd.edu/spacegrant/contacts/directors

/dir_directors.html. Those who are interested in applying may inquire at the state level, as awardees must be enrolled at the institution that will disburse the funds.

Job Settings

Most pilot astronauts and mission specialists work at the Johnson Space Center. Other NASA space centers include Ames Research Center, Moffett Field, California; Dryden Flight Research Center in California's Mojave Desert; Glenn Research Center, Lewis Field, Cleveland, Ohio; Goddard Space Flight Center, Greenbelt, Maryland; the Jet Propulsion Laboratory operated by the California Institute of Technology, Pasadena, California; Kennedy Space Center, Florida; Langley Research Center, Hampton, Virginia; Marshall Space Flight Center, Huntsville, Alabama; and Stennis Space Center, Bay Saint Louis, Mississippi.

Salaries for Astronauts

Astronauts begin their salaries in accordance with the U.S. government pay scale at GS-11 or 12 (approximately $45,000 to $53,000) status and may advance to GS-15 (approximately $87,000 to $113,000).

A Close-Up Look at the Profession

Following is a firsthand account from someone you may be familiar with—a celebrated member of the elite league of astronauts.

James Arthur Lovell Jr., Astronaut. As a high school junior, James Arthur Lovell Jr., with the help of a chemistry teacher and two friends, launched a rocket. Though it rose only eighty feet in the air and was only partially successful, Lovell knew even then that he longed for a career in rocket science.

True to his ambition, Lovell became a navy test pilot and was chosen to be an astronaut in 1962. He served as module pilot for the *Apollo 8* mission (the first manned flight to orbit the moon) and as a member of the *Gemini 7* crew (in space for two weeks). He also worked with pilot Edwin "Buzz" Aldrin on *Gemini 12* and served as commander of *Apollo 13* in 1970. The *Apollo 13* mission was very nearly a disaster when an explosion caused the shuttle to lose oxygen and power. For four days, the world waited and prayed that somehow the astronauts would make it back home safely.

The story of the *Apollo 13* mission was made into a movie based upon Lovell's book, originally titled *Lost Moon*. The box-office success starred Tom Hanks playing the part of James Lovell. To become familiar with the details, Hanks traveled to meet and fly with Lovell a year before making the film. "I tried to convey my feelings, actions, views, goals, and inner being to him, so he could gain some insights and a perception of the character," explains Lovell.

"I loved my career so much that, to tell you the truth, I would have worked for NASA for nothing," says Lovell. "It was such an amazing and interesting job. And I wasn't the only one who felt this way. So did most of the other astronauts and a lot of other people who worked for NASA. The attrition rate at the time was almost zero because no one wanted to leave. That's because the sense of achievement and satisfaction you receive as an astronaut for a job well done is incredible—pioneering new avenues, new vistas, seeing things for the first time. *Apollo 8* was an awe-inspiring flight because my mission mates and I were the first to see the far side of the moon. So it's obviously one of the great milestones of my career."

Lovell lists the qualities he believes a successful astronaut must possess: "Curiosity, the ability to handle stress, the facility to work well in team situations, the initiative to see problems and overcome them, sufficient training in a particular discipline such as biology or engineering, and the ability to perform optimally with only five or six hours of sleep per night! It's also important to be goal oriented and persistent. You need to be the kind of person who is motivated to stretch to accomplish goals and be qualified and ready to enhance luck to make it work for you in the best way possible."

James Lovell believes in the space program and is confident that it will have a future. "No matter what, I feel NASA will continue its efforts because it has proven to be a viable, creative program," Lovell says. "Funding will fluctuate up and down, and the numbers of people involved may vary, but it will always attract well-qualified individuals who are motivated to explore new worlds and share in the thrill of learning things we never knew before."

For Additional Information

Visit the NASA website to learn more about career opportunities and NASA's many programs: www.nasa.gov.

About the Author

Jan Goldberg's love for the printed page began well before her second birthday. Regular visits to the book bindery where her grandfather worked produced a magic combination of sights and smells that she carries with her to this day.

Childhood was filled with composing poems and stories, reading books, and playing library. Elementary and high school included an assortment of contributions to school newspapers. While a full-time college student, Goldberg wrote extensively as part of her job responsibilities in the College of Business Administration at Roosevelt University in Chicago. After receiving a degree in elementary education, she was able to extend her love of reading and writing to her students.

Goldberg has written extensively in the occupations area for *Career World Magazine*, as well as for the many career publications produced by CASS Communications. She has also contributed to a number of projects for educational publishers, including Free Spirit Publishing, Capstone Publishing, Publications International, Scott Foresman, Addison-Wesley, and Camp Fire Boys and Girls.

As a feature writer, Goldberg has published work in *Parenting*, *Today's Chicago Woman*, *Chicago Parent*, *Correspondent*, *Opportunity Magazine*, *Successful Student*, *Complete Woman*, *North Shore Magazine*, and the Pioneer Press newspapers. In all, she has published more than three hundred pieces as a full-time freelance writer.

In addition to *Careers for Patriotic Types and Others Who Want to Serve Their Country*, she is the author of fifteen other career books published by McGraw-Hill.

CAYUGA COMMUNITY COLLEGE
3 2551 00164874 4
County Community College